Cabinets of Curiosities

With essays by
Diane Douglas, Michelle Holzapfel,
Ursula Ilse-Neuman, Brock Jobe,
Tom Loeser, and Rick Mastelli

Wood Turning Center and The Furniture Society

This book is published on the occasion of the exhibition *Cabinets of Curiosities*, organized by
the Wood Turning Center, Philadelphia, and The Furniture Society, Asheville, North Carolina.

Exhibition Schedule
The Academy of Natural Sciences, Philadelphia, presented *Seven Wonders*
From March 24 to April 25, 2003

The Clay Studio, Philadelphia, presented *Holon Form*
From March 31 to April 25, 2003

Independence Visitor Center, Philadelphia, presented *Time Standing Still*
From March 31 to April 25, 2003

Franklin Institute, Philadelphia, presented *Ein Kleiner Wunderschrank (micro thaumata)*;
Givin' Adolf His Props; *Round Guy Meets Square Guy*; and *Cirque de Cabinet*
From March 28 to April 25, 2003

Albert M. Greenfield School, Philadelphia, presented *"Figurati . . ." ("go figure yourself")* and *Football*
From March 12 to April 25, 2003

Wood Turning Center, Philadelphia, Pennsylvania
May 2—July 26, 2003

Southern Alleghenies Museum of Art, Ligonier, Pennsylvania
September 2003—November 2003

Southern Alleghenies Museum of Art, Loretto, Pennsylvania
December 5, 2003—February 8, 2004

Houston Center for Contemporary Craft, Houston, Texas
April 6—May 25, 2004

Fuller Museum of Art, Brockton, Massachusetts
September 4—October 31, 2004

Leigh Yawkey Woodson Art Museum, Wausau, Wisconsin
November 20, 2004—January 23, 2005

Anchorage Museum of History and Art, Anchorage, Alaska
October 2—November 27, 2005

Erie Art Museum, Erie, Pennsylvania
December 17, 2005—March 26, 2006

The Society for Contemporary Craft, Pittsburgh, Pennsylvania
April 7—July 15, 2006

The exhibition and catalogue are made possible in part by Greater Philadelphia Marketing and Tourism Corporation,
The Independence Foundation, Penn State Industries, Pennsylvania Council on the Arts, Pennsylvania Humanities Council,
Philadelphia Cultural Fund, Samuel S. Fels Foundation, William Penn Foundation, Anne and Ronald Abramson,
Friends of The Furniture Society, and Friends of the Wood Turning Center.

The exhibition tour and publication are produced by the Wood Turning Center and The Furniture Society

Wood Turning Center
501 Vine Street, Philadelphia, PA 19106, Phone: 215.923.8000, Fax: 215.923.4403
www.woodturningcenter.org

The Furniture Society
111 Grovewood Road, Asheville, NC 28804, Phone: 828.255.1949, Fax: 828.255.1950
www.furnituresociety.org

Edited by Judson Randall, Portland, Oregon
Designed by Group M, Philadelphia
Photography by John Carlano, Philadelphia
Video segments produced by Rich Clark, Academy of Natural Sciences
Printed by Colorlith Corporation

Table of Contents

From the Wood Turning Center

The Curious Road From Concept to Traveling Exhibition: What, Who, and How

—Albert LeCoff
Executive Director

What—

One good idea often begets another—and another, and that's how this contemporary exhibition of curious objects and their personal cabinets evolved. Renowned wood sculptor Michelle Holzapfel, whose work shows her familiarity with containers and intriguing objects, brought a comprehensive vision for a cabinets of curiosities exhibition to me a number of years ago at the Wood Turning Center. She envisioned partners making cabinets and curious things to fill them, and that's what you'll see. Cross-fertilization among artists from different disciplines was important, not just traditional collaborators. Scholars and curators would bring context and critical analysis to the proposed work and the finished pieces, far from the times and original cultures where the traditions evolved. The public would enjoy venturing into the past while analyzing these contemporary interpretations of storage, containers, treasures, presentation and closure. This exhibition would provide the makers with a forum for exploring an age-old idea, and give the rest of us multiple visions with a perfectly contemporary spin.

Who—

Organizers

The Wood Turning Center took the cabinets concept to The Furniture Society. We were already working together to plan the 2003 Furniture Society conference in Philadelphia. We realized the cabinets proposal had the potential to draw both lathe artists and furniture makers. We wanted to inspire and nurture unusual collaborations between these two fields. The exhibition would also open with The Furniture Society's 2003 Conference. The cabinets would then travel, much as they had in other times and cultures.

Artists

The makers would rise to the challenge to create cabinets that would incorporate a collection of turned, built, or selected objects, unified by a theme. Their proposals would expand upon traditional approaches to safeguarding and displaying personal treasures. Would the makers be inspired to partner, to dream up concepts, and to present proposals so that they would be chosen to participate? What boundaries and horizons would they, the artists, perceive? Would they want to collaborate, construct, crate, and ship? What unexpected work would evolve? Turn the pages and see.

Curators

We sought experts to curate the proposals that would come in. We found a selection team who would consider the proposals within contexts larger than studio furniture and lathe arts. The selection team could help us explore and understand the many ways the makers might incorporate their ideas to alternately hide, and display the assorted curios. This included the selection process and the essays in this volume. These curators shaped the exhibition and shared their insights in this volume: Diane Douglas, founding executive director of a new Center for Liberal Arts at Bellevue Community College and former Director, Bellevue Art Museum, Bellevue, Washington; Brock Jobe, Professor of American Decorative Arts, Winterthur Museum, Winterthur, Delaware; Tom Loeser, Professor, Department of Art, University of Wisconsin, Madison, Wisconsin; Rick Mastelli, Editor, Photographer, Videographer, and principal of Image & Word, Montpelier, Vermont; Ursula Ilse-Neuman, Curator, Museum of Arts & Design, New York.

How—

The Selection Process

Over 90 artists submitted 57 proposals; each aimed to persuade the jurors that the artists could successfully execute their concept. The makers included painters, sculptors, ceramists, furniture makers, and wood workers, lathe turners, a sawyer, a hardware store employee, a photographer, and a bookmaker. The willing collaborators ranged from a six-year-old to two 80-year-old veteran wood workers. Drawings, models, resumes, and photographs of previous work supported the proposals. Some were rough, and some were finished. Intense deliberation and dialogue consumed two days. The jury agreed on 16 entries. This was a stretch because exhibitions are usually curated from finished pieces; the final entries were subject to the curators' approval of the finished pieces once they were shipped to Philadelphia.

Artists' Progress Reports

The artists had approximately 12 months to complete their cabinets. The work was grueling and two teams withdrew. Requisite mid-point progress reports included journals, photographs, samples, and a CD-ROM and video documenting stages of progress. Excerpts from these reports reflect the struggles of the creative process, and collaborating over distance and time.

Finished Products

The finished cabinets' arrival at a warehouse provided the perfect analogy for the exhibition. The locked storage unit held every variety of shipping crate. The voluminous crates protected the precious cabinets that held the curious contents. Opening the crates revealed the diverse cabinets. Unlatching, unlocking, or revolving, or sliding, or reversing various elements of the cabinets revealed their unique contents. Final inspections ensued; the curators, the warehouse staff, local museum staffs, and delighted children explored every nuance of the finished pieces. Now it's your turn.

From The Furniture Society

Cabinets of Curiosities

—Andrew H. Glasgow
Executive Director

Cabinets of Curiosities brings together two organizations and two disciplines in a show that ratifies the idea that collaboration can produce fine results. The Furniture Society and the Wood Turning Center are two non-profit organizations with similar missions, but with largely different audiences. And while the turned object and furniture have complemented and enhanced each other historically, they have evolved into separate spheres with their own store of traditions, stories, and fans. The *Cabinets of Curiosities* exhibition changes this perception. Co-sponsored by the Wood Turning Center and The Furniture Society, this exhibit reestablishes the creative bond between the contemporary turner and furniture maker with an exciting show that celebrates a collaboration of ideas, talent, and techniques. The work in *Cabinets of Curiosities* demonstrates that it's possible to have the best of both worlds.

The mission of The Furniture Society is to advance the art of studio furniture making by inspiring creativity, promoting excellence, and fostering understanding of this art and its place in society. *Cabinets of Curiosities* fulfills each aspect of our mission. The creative process between the artist teams is well documented and available to the viewer through a variety of media. To look at the objects in the exhibition, it is difficult to argue that the participants were not inspired by both the concept of the exhibition as well as the opportunity to work with their peers. This exhibition will travel for several years and be viewed by thousands during the run of the show. It is perhaps through this interaction between viewer and object that we gain the greatest understanding of furniture making and turning and how they relate.

There are several people who need to be thanked for their role in this exhibition. First among them is Albert LeCoff, the executive director of the Wood Turning Center. Albert was the driving force behind this exhibition, and it was through his able guidance that so much of the work was accomplished. The jurors, Diane Douglas, Ursula Ilse-Neuman, Brock Jobe, Rick Mastelli, and Tom Loeser, insured the quality of the show and the catalogue by bringing their valuable and informed points of view to the selection process. Brian Gladwell, the Society's President, provided guidance and oversight throughout the process, as did members of the exhibition committee. I also want to extend my appreciation to the makers who worked so diligently on this project, for without their endeavors, there would simply be no exhibition.

I am especially grateful that this exhibition provides The Furniture Society with an opportunity to strengthen its ties to Philadelphia and The Wood Turning Center, by fostering the occasion for these two communities of makers to work together. As you view the exhibition or read the catalogue, do so while knowing that what you see or hold is relatively rare in the modern era: makers from different communities working closely together to build and create a more exciting and complete object or product, an object or product that challenges and teaches us about the world in which we live.

Acknowledgments

—Fleur Bresler, President,
On behalf of the Wood Turning Center Board of Trustees

In 1984 at the invitation of the government of the Republic of China, my husband and I visited Taiwan to celebrate the country's National Day. While in Taipei we toured the National Palace Museum. It was at that time that I first saw a collection of "Cabinets of Curiosities." I was both fascinated and smitten. Years later when Michelle Holzapfel presented a proposal to the Wood Turning Center with Cabinets of Curiosities as the theme for a show, I was sold on the concept. As you will see in this catalogue the artists took the concept and ran with the idea. It is truly an innovative and a very special exhibition.

As we know, a show does not just happen. The Wood Turning Center and The Furniture Society distributed a joint prospectus. After the artists were chosen, the show was scheduled to coincide with both The Furniture Society's 2003 Conference in Philadelphia and the "Furniture Philadelphia 2003: A Region-Wide Celebration."

The following organizations' financial support made this presentation possible: The Greater Philadelphia Marketing and Tourism Corporation, Pennsylvania Council on the Arts, Pennsylvania Humanities Council, Samuel S. Fels Foundation, Pennsylvania Historic and Museum Commission, The Independence Foundation, Philadelphia Cultural Fund, Penn State Industries, William Penn Foundation, Anne and Ronald Abramson, Friends of The Furniture Society, and Friends of the Wood Turning Center.

Many individuals contributed their time and talents to bring this exhibition to fruition. Albert LeCoff, Executive Director of the Wood Turning Center; Andrew Glasgow, Executive Director of The Furniture Society; Kristine Allouchery, Wood Turning Center Administrator; and Hsiao-Ning Tu, Wood Turning Center Exhibition/Collections/Facility Coordinator. John Carlano photographed the objects for this publication; Anita Bassie and Tom Sokol of Group M designed this catalogue. Rachel Zimmerman and her staff at InLiquid.com designed and developed the various PR material and regional web site, Gabriel Romeu managed the Cabinets web site, and Richard D. Clark of The Academy of Natural Sciences produced the Cabinets CD-ROM.

Next to be recognized are the members of the Exhibitions committees of both the Wood Turning Center and The Furniture Society, and the Publications Committee of the Center. As individuals we are deeply indebted to Judson Randall, head of our Publications Committee who edited this publication and oversaw its production, and Michelle Holzapfel who originated the concept and brought it to the Center Exhibition Committee.

The *Cabinets of Curiosities* artists and curators have brought together a ground-breaking show. Each has provided extraordinary, insightful essays. They have spent numerous hours to complete this project. This exhibit has brought together artists from many diverse media and will certainly further the Wood Turning Center's mission of growth and awareness of the field of wood art.

I would like to extend our gratitude to all of the artists whose work brought about this exhibition, as well as all the artists who submitted their work for consideration. Without their dedication we would not be writing this today.

Lastly my gratitude to the Board of Trustees of the Wood Turning Center and the Board of Directors of The Furniture Society.

Thank you one and all.

Final Thoughts at the Beginning

—Michelle Holzapfel

**Artist, writer, member of Wood Turning Center
Exhibition Committee**

Michelle Holzapfel has more than two decades of experience
as an artist, turning and carving native hardwoods in Southern
Vermont where she lives. A graduate of Vermont College,
her work has been exhibited in museums and galleries in the
United States and Europe, and been acquired by the Museum
of Fine Arts in Boston, the Rhode Island School of Design
Museum, Yale University Art Gallery, the Smithsonian's
Renwick Gallery, and other public and private collections.
Ms. Holzapfel's work has been in many Wood Turning Center
exhibitions, including the first four *Challenge* exhibitions
through 1991. She was a co-curator of the Center's
*Challenge VI—Insights & Inspirations in Contemporary
Turned Objects*. Publications featuring her work include
House Beautiful, American Craft, Fine Woodworking and
Turning Points.

The collaborative cabinet I made for this exhibit is a structure of carved wooden books, housing an actual book that tells the story of its making. Likewise, this essay is the story of assembling a framework for the *Cabinets of Curiosities* exhibit; within it is housed the softer personal narrative of constructing a collaborative cabinet.

1995

It was a time of wild growth in the wood turning field. Conferences, symposia, and workshops were beginning to consider matters beyond "making the chips fly." I felt more welcome than ever to speak to the "why" of making things. It was a rare time of fluidity and ferment: Some collectors were turners, some turners made furniture, some furniture-makers derided turning, and some sophisticated art collectors (who'd never noticed contemporary turned objects before) were discovering the wood turning field. It was a moment ripe with potential for understanding, tension, and growth.

Since 1991, I'd been involved with Peter Joseph and his ambitious new (functional artfurniture? studiofurniture?) gallery in Manhattan. I felt somewhat out of place among heavyweights. I was the lone autodidact/woodcarving turner/vessel-maker. Now I threw myself into the deep end of the pool, trying my hand at constructing a suite of small boxes and cabinets for a solo show I entitled *Circling the Square*. Making things square necessitated the assistance of a friend, Dan MacArthur, whose cabinetmaking skills and equipment enabled my boxes to find form. This foray into collaboration reinforced how the power of alliance could help me expand the scope of my work.

I was also pursuing my long-deferred bachelor's degree. My studies proved to be a delicious condiment, spicing up long workdays of dust and woodchips with intervals of reading, writing and discussion. This fostered a broad range of reading opportunities, with great potential for that special delight—being ambushed by new words. You know how it is; you're reading along and suddenly there it is—"palimpsest," "schadenfreude," "grimoire"—a new word that seizes the eye and the mind and necessitates a trip to the dictionary. Inevitably, once I've encountered a new word, I suddenly begin seeing it everywhere.

That's how it happened, with the *wunderkammern*, the Cabinets of Curiosities. Just the sound of it— *cabinet*: three crisp syllables ending with the very square "t." A diminutive cabin, a den, a gallery. And *curiosities*: a twining, insinuating word; sounding like the shape of a questionmark; a condition that is its own cure. In the middle, the surprised "o." It killed the cat, but perhaps we'll escape with only singed eyebrows or a broken heart.

A Cabinet . . . plus Curiosities: Pandora's box.

I first encountered references to these *wunderkammern*, Cabinets of Curiosities, in my readings about the infancy of natural history museums during the "Age of Enlightenment." These personal collections—virtual proto-museums—strove to contain and describe the known world. Collectors harvested antiquities, natural specimens, and scientific instruments with all the arrogance, appetite, and enterprise of manic, expansive 17th-century Europe.

Other references to *wunderkammern* began popping up in broader and more idiosyncratic incarnations. A friend spoke of his visit to the Museum of Jurassic Technology in Los Angeles—a contemporary wunderkammern—which is wonderfully described in Lawrence Weschler's *Mr. Wilson's Cabinet of Wonder*. And several conversations with Susan Hagen established our mutual, independent encounters with this intriguing concept.

Figure 1
Michelle Holzapfel
Town + Country Box
1994
Walnut and basswood
11 x 17 x 11 in.
Private collection

Figure 2
Michelle Holzapfel
Pandora's Box
1995
Basswood
15 x 11 x 11 in.
Private collection

Enter my friend, Coincidence, with its power to catalyze seeming disparities into fruitfulness. I was attending an "Allturnatives" weekend workshop where I offered slidetalks on "the power of scale" and "getting a feeling for form." Fellow presenter (and polymath) Craig Nutt and I exchanged thoughts and jokes about both the connections and tensions between wood turning and furniture making. Weren't these allied skills—why the fraternal friction? I began to think about what could reconcile them . . . the cabinet, of course. The realm of my studies and the world of my work were coming together with a magnetic click, like the closing of a well-hung cabinet door. This cabinet idea could be translated for today's makers, and reinvented as a multi-functional organizing principle: reconciliation through collaboration.

After the conference, driving back to Philly with Albert LeCoff, I vented about my Cabinets of Curiosities idea—though "idea" is too neat a word for those tangled strands of conjecture and enthusiasm. Yet the idea piqued Albert's curiosities . . . he scented the potential. Here are some excerpts from my first draft. (Remember, I was in college.)

Cabinets Of Curiosities
Introduction

In the world-view of the Renaissance, the belief in the bond between art, nature, and Divinity found expression in the personal collections referred to as wunderkammern, or "cabinets of curiosities." Since the heyday of these cabinets—from c. 1550 to 1750—the activity of collecting has continuously evolved.

The Renaissance cabinets often filled vast rooms or entire buildings. However, this more modest proposal would assemble a limited set of cabinets that would be easy to move and also serve as the containers for the collections of (turned?) objects within them. This exhibit would be a collection of collections.

Artists could work independently or collaborate: A cabinetmaker with a theme in mind could invite turning artists to make objects for a cabinet. A group of artists could make turned objects based on a theme and commission a cabinetmaker to create a cabinet specifically for their work. An artist may wish to make both a cabinet and its contents—a one-person show in miniature.

1996

While participating in a Wood Turning Center retreat, I was exposed to the spectrum of needs, tensions, and interrelations among all the Center's stakeholders: galleries, patrons and artists, amateurs and pros, teachers, curators, and the Center's staff. The cabinet idea was still simmering on the back burner, and this retreat offered a fresh viewpoint from which to reconsider my original proposal. During a breakfast conversation with Stephen Hogbin and Ken Trapp, I floated my nascent proposal. Their knowledgeable enthusiasm both encouraged and sobered me. It was an intriguing, overambitious, sprawling, and unwieldy proposition containing much potential and even more questions.

How could I re-frame this democratization of the personal "museum" into a cogent, succinct call for entries? Could the C. of C. still fulfill its original purpose—to describe and contain a microcosm of the maker's world? Could it be argued that the ubiquitous personal computer, coupled with the sprawling, virtual mother-of-all-cabinets—The Internet—already served this purpose? Would a contemporary version of a 17th-century European phenomenon be interpreted as a facile "Museum of Me?" And how could this proposal be tailored to meet the practical limitations of a travelling exhibit reflecting the field today? Using the mission statement of the WTC as a template, I redrafted my proposal.

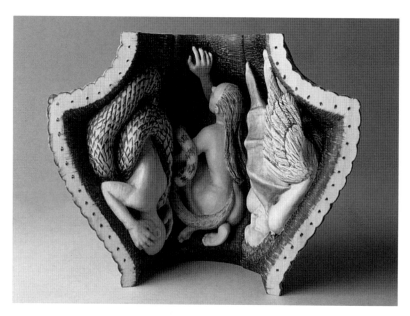

Figure 2 (detail)
Michelle Holzapfel
Pandora's Box

Here's a part of that second working draft:

Cabinets of Curiosities

To create a collection of small cabinets, each containing collections of objects, unified by a theme to be determined by the makers.

To create documentation specific to each cabinet and its contents. This will provide educational support and encourage understanding of technique, material, process, design, function, collaboration, imagery, and/or historical tradition.

To foster integration, cooperation, and reconciliation among groups often isolated, alienated, or at odds: turners and furniture makers, autodidacts and academics, functional/production turners, and decorative/sculptural turners.

To cultivate the spirit of curiosities—for makers and their audiences. To showcase the range and diversity of the dynamic processes, the invisible helpers, and the inner workings of our field.

The network for this enterprise already exists; this exhibit would strengthen it.

After several more drafts—with help from Susan Hagen, Stephen Hogbin and other members of the Exhibitions Committee—the idea was close to being launched, like a child's toy boat zigzagging its way along a spring stream. As Fate would have it, Philadelphia would be hosting The Furniture Society conference in 2003, and the Wood Turning Center envisioned the society's partnership in sponsoring the Cabinets of Curiosities show. It was a natural alliance that could draw a wide range of participants. The final draft of the call for entries emphasized the allure of the personal collection and the synergistic collaboration between turners and furnituremakers.

At this point, I was ready to step away from the process of organizing the exhibit. It would take its own institutional trajectory. I was already beginning to formulate my own proposal for a cabinet.

1998

David and I attended a "Breaking Barriers" event at Emma Lake, Saskatchewan. We played a small part in a hilarious and serious working sprint with Craig Nutt and others. Besides being an invigorating break from our studio work, the experience reinforced my hope that the cabinet collaborations would be charged with the same vitality, spirit, and fertility as our short Canadian adventure.

2001

During the course of the many drafts of the Cabinets of Curiosities proposal I had traversed an all-too-familiar terrain from the land of free-flowing ideas and sweeping concepts through the journey of a thousand small steps to a finished product.

Now, several years later, David and I arrived at two different cabinet proposals. We both wanted to work with Craig Nutt again. Out of many conversations and e-mails came what I thought of as the Interstate Divination Cabinet. It would contain collections of objects to help sort out one's angst-ridden life: Ouija board, Magic 8-ball, perhaps some carved wooden chicken entrails? We were also grappling with the sober, practical considerations of where and when and how to actually get it done. Travel was expensive; time was short. And as much fun as it was bandying ideas for this cabinet, it ultimately proved perhaps too free-wheeling in spirit for the panel of jurors. I'd venture to say that some of the best cabinets in this exhibit never got made—but shined gloriously in our imaginations. Yet the sheer pleasure of indulging in grandiose dreamweaving was the truest compensation for the hard work that followed.

My more conservative proposal—David and I in collaboration with local artisans—was accepted. As it turned out, even this practical and modest hometown proposal would prove to be more than enough of a challenge for all involved.

We embarked upon our trek with an orderly statement of intent:

· Our cabinet will be a microcosmic museum which can appeal to a wide range of viewers whose curiosities will sustain the unpacking of the cabinet. It will consist of a trompe l'oeil carved stack of books and two hollow book/boxes. One will open to reveal a hand-bound photo album, and the second will hold a guest book.

· The album will illustrate the skills of design, carving, cabinetry, bookmaking, photography, and narrative. It will document the technical processes used to make the book/box—from tree to cabinet, and will include photographic portraits and brief profiles of the collaborators. The guest book will record the comments of viewers and will become part of the documentation of the cabinet's provenance.

2002

The conception and construction of our local collaborative cabinet traversed the familiar paths of brainstorming, banter, and sustained labor. The collaboration was mainly among three of us: Donna Hawes, as a maker of books; David Holzapfel in his capacity as a photographer; and me as woodworker. In addition to our commitment to the Cabinet project, Donna has two young children, David is a full-time teacher, and I was preparing for a solo show in the fall of 2002. We began meeting in July; we shipped the finished piece just before Thanksgiving.

The final form of the cabinet and its documentation are close to identical to our original proposal. What will never be seen, however, are the many delightful ideas, details and helpers that were a part of this piece—only in our imaginations.

A recurrent motif in our collaboration was the process's logistical circularity. How large to make the book/box depended on the format of the album, which depended on the format of the photo images. How many pages depended upon how many images of the process. And we wouldn't have all the process images until the piece was finished. So we couldn't even start until we estimated how large to make the book/box.

From this fog of indecision, the angel of limitation appeared. I knew I wanted to use some of the excellent four-inch-thick well seasoned basswood that I had stashed for just such a purpose. The limits of its dimensions mercifully dictated our album format. Donna selected, sized, and stacked the sturdy album pages until they reached the desired thickness of two inches: forty sheets. That's what we'd work with, and we'd just edit the images to fit. Already we knew that much of the story would end up on the floor.

Throughout the fall, we negotiated the minefields of conflicting schedules, shrinking deadlines, and technical and physical limitations. Trudging the territory between grand idea and knuckle-scraping reality, we recognized that much of our process couldn't be documented: the encyclopedia got pared down to a guidebook. Many aspects of our dream-cabinet were reluctantly dropped. The oral history component —interviews with the participants on a CD—was a serious problem. Would we embed a CD player and earphones into the cabinet? The CD idea was abandoned.

The participation of an eccentric local machinist was problematic. Images of his machine shop— still functioning with its bewildering overhead belts and driveshafts—would have been terrific, but our cabinet didn't require any custom-machined parts. Plus, he was a notoriously charming procrastinator. We didn't need any more variables—so we consigned this facet to the realm of the could-have-been. Then, we had hoped to have our town's doyenne of bookbinding, Ellen Becker, help with some gilding and leather-tooling. But she was ill with pneumonia, so her participation was shelved.

Nonetheless, this cabinet would still be a microcosm of our world—the local community of craftspeople and enterprises that enables and supports our efforts. When I had made some boxes in the mid-'90s, I had collaborated with our good friend and post-and-beam builder, Dan MacArthur. He had the jointers and planers and a wealth of suggestions for putting things together. Although his contributions to the cabinet would be minimal, I was glad to have the weight of his experience as ballast to my flights.

The greatest delights are always the surprises, most of which came in the interviews for the short profiles we included. David spent a working day on the skidder with a logger, Kim Thayer (who's been playing skidder since the age of five). We learned that our sawyer's daughter was an acrobat in the Cirque de Soleil, and discovered more of the history of our beloved local family-owned hardware store, Brown and Roberts.

It was a great pleasure to work with Donna Hawes. Witnessing the processes of making a book—enjoying the sheer sensual delight of the fabrics and leather and handmade papers—deepened my abiding love of the book as a form. In turn, I introduced her to the virtues of the Forstner bit. We learned a lot from each other. And as always, David's steady dedication to the project—camera at the ready—yielded so many vivid images with which to tell our story. Take a careful look at the faces in the 4 x 5 portraits of the collaborators: Their openness and honesty reflect their trust in and affection for the person behind the lens.

The weekend before Thanksgiving, we finished and launched our offering, inviting participants, friends, and neighbors to be the first to sign the cabinet's guestbook. In the end, the community that so steadily supports our work took on a brighter, sharper, weightier presence through the process of building our cabinet. Although most books place the Acknowledgment at the back, I chose to place it at the beginning of our book:

Acknowledgment
is at the heart of this project.
David's photographs tell the story of how
Michelle made the cabinet and Donna made the books.
It also serves as a record of the collaboration with other people:
family, friends, neighbors, and business associates.
This is only the beginning of the cabinet's story.
You, the viewers, are invited to participate in this Cabinet of Curiosities
and contribute to its history.

2003
So here I am at the end of my work and at the beginning of the exhibit. I'm grateful for the opportunity to offer my version of the history of an idea. This essay stands as the other bookend, the far parenthesis, bracketing almost a decade from the first faint flutters of a fledgling idea to the beginning of the exhibit as a reality. I offer profound thanks to all who supported and nurtured the Idea. And I look forward to seeing the other 13 interpretations of the Cabinets of Curiosities.

Whose curiosities will be kindled and satisfied? I wonder.

Cabinets of Wonder and Delight

—Ursula Ilse-Neuman

Curator, Museum of Arts & Design, New York

Ursula Ilse-Neuman is curator at the Museum of Arts & Design (formerly, American Craft Museum) in New York City. She has organized major exhibitions, including the retrospective *Made In Oakland: The Furniture of Garry Knox Bennett*. She is currently preparing the Ninth Triennial, *Corporal Identity*, in collaboration with the Museum of Applied Arts in Frankfurt, Germany.

Ms. Ilse-Neuman is the author of numerous publications, and she lectures widely. She is currently a Ph.D. candidate at the Bard Graduate Center for Studies in the Decorative Arts, Design, and Culture. Her professional affiliations include the International Curators Association, The Furniture Society, Art Table, and the American Museum Association.

The masterfully crafted works on display in Cabinets of Curiosities *are superb examples of the integration of art and ideas. Sophisticated in concept and execution, they are in their own way as revelatory as Renaissance curiosity cabinets were in their time, evoking a sense of inquisitiveness and wonder. These contemporary masterpieces cause us to marvel at man's eternal drive to express his highest thoughts and feelings—all that he knows of himself and his place in the cosmos—through artistic creations.*

Interest in collecting and displaying the unusual and mysterious has a long history that reaches well back into Antiquity.[1] It was during the great Age of Curiosity, from 1450 to 1700, however, that an unprecedented enthusiasm swept across Europe to collect rare and extraordinary objects of art, nature, and human invention.[2] First organized in dedicated rooms (*Kammern*) of art (*Kunst*) and marvels (*Wunder*), these wide-ranging collections were later displayed in unique cabinets that achieved their most elaborate expression in the Augsburg *Kunstschrank* of Philipp Hainhofer (1578–1647) in early 17th-century southern Germany.

Rooms filled with wondrous treasures (*Wunderkammern*) reflected the spirit of Renaissance Europe, when curiosity, which previously had been stigmatized and criticized by the Church in the Middle Ages, became a virtue. During this period, the insular and theologically ordained perspective of the Middle Ages was transformed into a more secular world view characterized by a spirit of inquisitiveness and a thirst for knowledge that both fostered and was fostered by exploration and scientific discovery. The latter half of the 15th century marked the beginning of great economic expansion as the ravages of the plague known as the Black Death receded, cities grew, and voyages of discovery and trade shifted Europe's focus from the Mediterranean to the Atlantic and beyond.[3]

During this time, collectors acquired "curiosities" to showcase the breadth of their erudition and humanist learning, as well as their social status. More than a random assemblage, collections were customarily organized into three classes of objects: *Naturalia* (products of nature), which incorporated natural specimens, minerals, fossils, botanical items (such as fruits, nuts, and dried plants), and zoological items (stuffed animals, horns, teeth, shells, eggs, and skins), as well as monstrosities, abnormalities and the misshapen;[4] *Artefacta* or *Artificialia* (products of man), which included paintings (often portraits of the collector's ancestors), graphic work (copper engravings, woodcuts, drawings and watercolors), sculpture, works by gold- and silversmiths, textiles, jewelry, coins and medals, small pieces of furniture, books, and documents, as well as exotica from distant lands; and *Scientifica* (objects testifying to man's growing ability to understand and control nature), including astrolabes, clocks, automatons, and scientific instruments, as well as medical paraphernalia and pharmaceuticals.

Collecting became part of the social fabric of aristocratic circles throughout Europe and famous families such as the Gonzagas and the Medicis in Italy,[5] and the Hapsburgs in Austria were renowned for their collections.[6] In many ways, these encyclopedic collections were the forerunners of the modern museum, yet they were generally accessible to only a select group of visitors and were never intended as a form of public learning. They were private sites where the physical manifestations of the whole of nature, brought together in microcosm, could be analyzed and comprehended in rooms dedicated for their enjoyment and study.[7] Collecting, cataloging, and organizing the objects was not an end in itself but an integral part of an ongoing process of self-discovery. As trade increased, owning a collection became more popular, and soon humanist scholars, lawyers, physicians, and even tavern owners competed to acquire the unusual and bizarre.[8]

Figure 3
Curiosity Cabinet of Ferrante Imperator
c. 1600
Palazzo Gravina, Naples

The age was marked by an astonishing amount of personal travel as well, despite its hardships and hazards. Travelers were welcome throughout Europe, and in Rome and Paris even beggars made their appeals in several languages as a well-dressed stranger approached.[9] Sir Francis Bacon noted in 1626: "The things to be seen are: the courts of princes, the courts of justice, the churches, the monuments, walls, and fortifications, harbors, antiquities, ruins, and libraries, colleges, shipping and navies, houses and gardens, armories and arsenals, exchanges, warehouses, exercises of horsemanship, fencing, and training of soldiers, comedies of the better sort, treasuries of jewels, robes, and rarities, as well as triumphs, masques, feasts, weddings, and capital executions."[10]

The origin of special collecting rooms in the 15th century can be traced back to medieval armories and treasuries where crown jewels were kept. A more humanistic and scholarly emphasis was expressed in the Italian *studiolo* or *museo*, where collections of art and paintings were placed beginning in the 14th century.[11] The humanist studiolo of 15th-century Italy included objects of curiosity and was designed to interweave a sense of wonder with intellectual and scientific study, capturing the period's interest in the past and also in contemporary discoveries that were changing the world view. Possessing a studiolo as a place of study and refuge was associated with concepts of civility and taste and reflected the increasing sense of individualism at the time.[12]

The more elaborate, princely collections of the 16th century were housed in a series of interconnected rooms, each dedicated to a particular field of collecting. These rooms were frequently organized according to a philosophy that subdivided the world into fours: the four continents (Europe, Asia, America, and Africa), the four elements (earth, water, fire, and air), the four human temperaments (melancholic, sanguine, choleric, and phlegmatic), the four cardinal directions, and the four seasons. The rooms themselves were designed to incorporate a diversity of objects, including globes, clocks, mechanical devices, caskets, mirrors, and musical instruments, as well as tables, chests, and, most notably, writing desks. Jewelry cases and boxes were also kept in these chambers and stood independently in the room if they were large or were kept hidden inside a cabinet or chest if they were small. Over the decades, these rooms were designed with integrated furnishings, some fitted with box-type closets and a bench and writing desk fixed to a platform to make it more stable and to keep the scholar's feet off the cold floor. By the end of the 16th century in Northern Europe, special rooms for housing curiosities, the Wunderkammer, and special rooms for housing art, the Kunstkammer, had merged into Kunst- und Wunderkammern, and nearly all German courts boasted one.[13]

Following the appearance of special rooms for the display of collections, a specially designed furniture form, the "curiosity cabinet," evolved. Typologically, the curiosity cabinet had elements derived from the writing desk, the coin cabinet, and the jewelry box, with origins that can be traced to Moorish Spain. Its development began about 1500 with two forms: the *cofre de Valencia*, which resembled a chest, with a door on one side concealing several small drawers, and the *escritorio*, a table-chest whose front could be opened to serve as a writing surface. The Italian writing desk (*scrittorio*), which was modeled after the escritorio, introduced such new features as a roof-like top and intarsia work on the front, which personalized the cabinets according to the specific tastes of the patron.

Many different craftsmen were involved in the adornment of these cabinets: the gold- and silversmith; the lapidary cutter of cameos; the ivory engraver; the painter; the sculptor and bronze worker; and the embroiderer. Their interiors grew in richness and complexity, and the entire cabinet often

Figure 4
Philipp Hainhofer
Pomeranian Kunstschrank
1610–16
140 x 93 x 85 cm.
Staatliche Museen zu Berlin-Preussischer
Kulturbesitz Kunstgewerbemuseum

resembled a miniature palace concealing secret drawers and compartments, further enhancing the revelatory quality of the cabinet and challenging the virtuosity of the cabinetmaker's art.

In the hands of German artists and craftsmen in the late 16th century, the curiosity cabinet, or Kunstschrank, changed dramatically into a sumptuous work constructed of such exotic woods as ebony, pear, and amaranth; embellished with precious materials including ivory, mother-of-pearl, marble, and alabaster; and further ornamented with gilding, silver mounts, and fittings with elaborate locks. The Kunstschrank was considered a miniature version of the Wunderkammer, and collectors were actively involved in the design of their own cabinets and in the selection of the themes to be depicted by the artists and craftsmen. By the 17th century, these virtuoso masterpieces had made German craftsmanship and scholarship renowned throughout Europe, and the southern German cities of Nuremberg and Augsburg were exporting Kunstschränke made to order as diplomatic presentation pieces or as gifts to be exchanged between kings and princes.

The German merchant, collector, and diplomat Philipp Hainhofer was one of the most important figures in the construction and spread of the renowned Augsburg Kunstschrank. He was a passionate collector with contacts in many European countries who helped him track down desired objects. He provided several courts with news of discoveries that he made at markets, fairs, or in collectors' private homes. After founding his own textile enterprise in Augsburg in 1601, following studies in Padua, Cologne, and the Netherlands, Hainhofer began designing complex and intricate curiosity cabinets that contained collections he had compiled. Hainhofer manufactured these Kunstschränke at his own risk, hoping to sell them with their contents to princely collectors.[14]

Hainhofer was the perfect man for his age. Not only was he attracted to the artifacts of the past, he also kept abreast of the crosscurrents in contemporary thought that were sweeping across Europe. More importantly, he had the ability to express this dramatically changing world view in precious curiosity cabinets.

Hainhofer supervised the construction of four large curiosity cabinets in Augsburg in the first half of the 17th century, the last of which was built in 1643. The *Stipo Tedesco*, now in the Museo degli Argenti in the Pitti Palace in Florence, Italy, was constructed from 1619 to 1626 and purchased by Archduke Leopold V of Austria, whose wife, Claudia de Medici, subsequently presented it to her nephew, Grand Duke Ferdinand II of Tuscany. Duke August von Braunschweig-Lüneburg purchased Hainhofer's last Kunstschrank shortly before Hainhofer's death in 1647 and presented it as a lavish diplomatic gift to Field Marshal Count Carl Gustav Wrangel (1613–1676), the commander of the Swedish army in Germany. The cabinet, without its contents, is in the Kunsthistorisches Museum in Vienna. Two of the finest and best documented are the Pomeranian cabinet and the Uppsala cabinet, the latter being the one that still has its original collection virtually intact.

The first of Hainhofer's masterworks was the so-called Pomeranian Kunstschrank, begun in 1610 as a commission from Philip, Duke of Pomerania-Stettin, and completed around 1616, shortly before the outbreak of the Thirty Years War. Made of ebony, palissandre, rosewood, silver parcel-gilt, enamel, and precious stones, it took nearly seven years to complete and cost the astronomical sum of 20,000 thalers, the price of over seven hundred ordinary saddle horses. The Pomeranian Kunstschrank was destroyed in World War II, but its contents of silverware, paintings, games, instruments, tools, and pharmaceutical items are now housed in the Kunstgewerbemuseum in Berlin.

Figure 5
Philipp Hainhofer
Uppsala Kunstschrank
1625–31
240 x 120 x 120 cm.
Uppsala University Art Collections, Sweden

The Pomeranian Kunstschrank was built by cabinetmaker Ulrich Baumgartner (c. 1580–1652) to a design by Hans Rottenhammer and Matthias Kager (1566–1634)[15] and was the product of over thirty craftsmen and artists from fifteen different guilds, all of whom worked under Hainhofer's supervision.[16] Each material in the cabinet was worked by a specialist whose tools were added, in miniature, to the content of the cabinet, together with writing implements, mathematical-astronomical instruments, games, and clocks.

Hainhofer planned its contents so that the entire piece would constitute a harmonious whole in which form and function were integrated through the cabinet's physical construction, through the mythological and allegorical themes that constituted its decoration, and through the objects it housed.[17] Hainhofer's design prominently featured shell-like ornamentation and silver inlays illustrating scholarship, mathematics, and painting, which served as a visual key to the contents within.

Prominently positioned at the center of the Stettin Kunstkammer, between the existing displays of *naturalia* and *artificialia*, the Pomeranian Kunstschrank joined with the other elements in the room to constitute an "encyclopedia of the physical and moral world."[18] The Pomeranian cabinet was a splendid example of the Kunstschrank as a miniature Wunderkammer and as a symbol of a world view that was rooted in a compelling curiosity to unlock mysteries through an understanding and appreciation of art and science. Depictions of religious themes were almost entirely absent. Instead, the nine muses on the top of the cabinet highlighted the liberal arts, with the Parnassus at the apex symbolizing the fields of art and science. The four elements were prominently featured, and one of the doors is decorated with a painting entitled *die Erde* (the Earth), a portrayal of various human explorations of the earth, including craftsmen[19] and miners working with precious minerals and transforming them into artworks, a statement of the dignity of labor and craft.

The Pomeranian cabinet contained a wide range of instruments and tools that represent the physical world and the triumph of human ingenuity and science over nature, an idea that was intimately related to the underlying philosophy of the Kunstkammer, and one that was manifested by uniting artificial and natural objects, much in the same fashion that a goldsmith would embellish a Nautilus shell or ostrich egg.

In his description of the Kunstschrank, Hainhofer stressed that its function was also to entertain, and the cabinet housed various parlor games, chessboards, and sets of playing cards, on the backs of which were written the melodies of thirteen popular love songs. With a size that was not imposing, it was an intricate treasure chest to be explored, pored over, and used for many hours and days.

The Uppsala Kunstschrank was made between 1625 and 1631 at a cost of 6,500 thalers and was presented in 1632 to Gustavus Adolphus, the great warrior king of Sweden, by the citizens of Augsburg.[20] It survives virtually intact in the Chancellor's Room at Uppsala University, except for its original numismatic collection, which was dispersed and its description lost. Sumptuously decorated with miniatures and inlays in fine woods, precious metals, and minerals, with numerous compartments that open in unexpected ways, the Uppsala cabinet contains an overwhelming number of curious artifacts and exotic *naturalia*. It is a museum in miniature and a reflection of the contemporary world view.

The iconography of the cabinet represents the animal, plant, and mineral kingdoms, the four known continents, the four seasons, and all known epochs of history. Although the themes are decidedly secular, the cabinet's paintings represent a "compendium of all Holy scripture," with biblical scenes ranging from Genesis to Revelations. The depiction of love in many guises appears repeatedly in the paintings, and this theme is accentuated by the cabinet's crowning statue of Venus. Contemporary events

Figure 5 (detail)
Philipp Hainhofer
Uppsala Kunstschrank

are duly acknowledged, including scenes of the outbreak of the Thirty Years War in Augsburg. Small paintings on ivory at the corners of the cabinet show beautiful faces that transmogrify into grinning skulls when turned upside down, the so-called *Verkehrsbilder*, reflecting a fascination with the grotesque and mysterious. Silver animals cast from nature in the *style rustique* are included as well as a mechanically automated scene of Apollo and Cyparissus changing into a cypress tree. The most striking part of the Uppsala cabinet is its crowning feature: a boat-shaped ewer formed from a rare Seychelles nut in a gilt mount chased with shells, crabs, tortoises, and other sea creatures. It stands in a lush garden of red, white, and black coral branches, shells, and crystals created by Augsburg specialists skilled in imitating nature.

The Uppsala Kunstschrank was also designed to amuse and entertain, offering a deck of cards, a chess set, and other parlor games, along with distorting mirrors and a variety of spectacles. The cabinet even contained practical jokes, such as two pairs of gloves sewn together so that they could not be worn, artificial eggs, halves of nuts with illusionistic insects, a mug that cannot be drunk from, and, hidden in a "mountain," an automaton with moving figures that perform a scene from Ovid's *Metamorphoses*. Among its greatest wonders is an Italian spinet from about 1600 incorporating an automatic playing mechanism that still affords a unique opportunity to hear early baroque music. A medicine cabinet, together with simple cosmetic and toiletry paraphernalia, was also available, including a small basin made of silver in which Queen Christina may have washed her hands.

Kunstschränke were frequently kept secret and only shown to a select number of people. Furthermore, many of the objects inside the Kunstschrank were hidden in secret compartments or drawers, a practice that reveals something about how "knowledge" was perceived at the time and how it was supposed to be guarded and disseminated. This form of secrecy, namely the intentional suppression of knowledge to protect it from abuse, fell within the traditions of esotericism and hermeticism, which had been the basis for medieval alchemy as well as for various magical/mystical orders. It may also allude to secret mystical, religious reform movements such as Rosicrucianism that developed in Germany in the early 17th century.[21] On an epistemological level, the notion of secrecy also implied the unknowable in nature.

In the 16th- and 17th-century Kunstschrank, seemingly disparate objects, such as a pinecone and a pineapple, might be placed next to one another to evoke associations and memories. As such, the design philosophy of the Kunstschrank may have been influenced by the Theater of Memories (*Teatro della Memoria*) invented by Giulio Camillo Delmino (1480–1544), one of the 16th century's most prominent thinkers, who was, nevertheless, completely forgotten by the 18th. Camillo's theater, an actual wooden structure first constructed in Venice and then in Paris, was the talk of Europe at the time and remained so well after his death when his *L'idea del Theatro* was published in 1584. His theater continued to exert a strong influence, notably in England, where its impact on two Elizabethan hermetic philosophers, John Dee (1527–1609) and Robert Fludd (1574–1637), may have helped shape Shakespeare's Globe Theatre.

Hainhofer's interest in mysticism may have been linked to that of Camillo, who had belonged to the Hermetic-kabbalistic tradition initiated by the Italian philosopher and scholar Pico della Mirandola (1463–1494).[23] There may well have been a connection between these philosophical currents and the Wunderkammern of the 16th and 17th centuries. The cabinets of curiosity were eclectic collections of oddities, displaying man-made objects inspired by the new sensibilities of science, along with contemporary works of art that were juxtaposed against exotic objects of natural history and supposed relics of religious significance, folklore, and antiquity. The "wonders of God" were systematically arrayed with the "wonders of man" and arranged in a series of tableaux on the cabinet, the examination of which would shock the viewer into a new conception of reality.

In their elaborate design and craftsmanship, the Kunstschränke of 17th-century Augsburg marked the high point for the curiosity cabinet, but they also marked the end of an era. Only a few wealthy collectors could afford such extreme costs in workmanship and materials, which led to a reaction against the grand formality of elaborate royal cabinets. Over time, the encyclopedic and esoteric collections of curiosities evolved into larger displays, many of which became the progenitors of the modern museum.[24]

[1] In his writings on the lives of the Caesars, the historian Suetonius (c. 69–122) describes Augustus's houses: "Those of his own, which were far from sumptuous, he adorned, not so much with statues and pictures, as with walks and groves, and things which were curious either for their antiquity or for rarity; such as, at Capri, the huge limbs of sea-monsters and wild beasts, which some affect to call the bones of giants; and also the arms of ancient heroes." Suetonius, *The Twelve Caesars*, Robert Graves (translator) (New York: Penguin Books, 1991), 98.

[2] The term "Age of Curiosity" was coined by French historian Krzysztof Pomian in his *Collectors and Curiosities: Paris and Venice, 1500–1800*, trans. Elizabeth-Wiles-Portier (London: Polity Press, 1990), 45–64. A more recent reassessment of this theme is in Lorraine Daston, "Curiosity in Early Modern Science," *Word and Image* 11 (1995): 391–404, and Lorraine Daston and Katharine Park, *Wonders and the Order of Nature 1150–1750* (New York: Zone Books, 1999).

[3] The Age of Exploration is exemplified by the voyages of Christopher Columbus (1451–1506) to the New World under Spanish auspices; the first English voyage around the world by Sir Francis Drake (c. 1540–1596); the first European voyage to India by Portugal's Vasco da Gama (c. 1460–1524), which also led to the exploration of the west coast of Africa; the discovery of the Cape of Good Hope by Bartolomeu Dias (c. 1450–1500); and Ferdinand Magellan's (1480–1521) circumnavigation of the globe.

[4] In France, King Charles V (reg. 1364–1380) and his brother Jean de France, duc de Berry (1340–1416) were among the first to establish collections of natural specimens and art objects at the end of the 14th century.

[5] Cosimo (1389–1464) and afterwards Lorenzo (1449–1492), de Medici were forward looking patrons of the new learning who inspired numerous other royal collections throughout Europe.

[6] As Holy Roman emperors, the Hapsburgs established one of the first Central European Kunstkammern in Innsbruck in the 16th century, with a lavish collection displayed in twenty cases and organized according to materials. The collection, much of which is now displayed in the Kunstkammer in the Kunsthistorishes Museum in Vienna, contained suits of armor, statues of Hapsburg ancestors, art objects, natural specimens and exotica, together with such works of human invention as automatons and complicated and peculiar scientific instruments and clocks.

[7] On the relationship between these different kinds of early collecting practices, see Horst Bredekamp, *The Lure of Antiquity and the Cult of the Machine: The Kunstkammer and the Evolution of Nature, Art and Technology*, trans. Allison Brown (Princeton, N. J.: Markus Wiener, 1995), and Paula Findlen, *A Fragmentary Past: Museums and the Renaissance* (Stanford, Calif,: Stanford University Press, 2000).

[8] Mark Meadow and Bruce Robertson, *Microcosms: Objects of Knowledge: A University Collects* (Santa Barbara, Calif: University of California, Santa Barbara, 1995)

[9] Jacques Barzun, *From Dawn to Decadence* (New York: Harper Collins, 2000), 81.

[10] Sir Francis Bacon, "Of Travel," as quoted in Barzun, op. cit., 80.

[11] The first *studiolo* is attributed to the Italian scholar and man of letters Francesco Petrarca (Petrarch) (1304–1374), who considered solitude to be the basis for all creative and intellectual endeavors.

[12] Dora Thornton, *The Scholar in His Study: Ownership and Experience in Renaissance Italy* (New Haven and London: Yale University Press, 1997), 146.

[13] The term *Kunst- und Wunderkammer* may have been used for the first time by Count Froben Christoph von Zimmern and his scribe Johannes Müller in their historical description *Zimmerische Chronik*, of 1564–66 (Meersburg/Leipzig: Karl Barack/Paul Herrmann, 1932), 2:578.

[14]Hainhofer sent letters in Latin, English, French, Italian, and German to princes all over Europe, including the kings of Denmark, Poland, Spain, England, and France, the Queen of France, the Duke of Orleans, Emperor Ferdinand II, Empress Maria Anna, and the Signoria of Genoa. Philipp Hainhofer lost his entire fortune in the Thirty Years War and died in poverty. Hans-Olof Boström: *Det underbara skåpet: Philipp Hainhofer och Gustav II Adolfs konstskåp* (Uppsala: Acta Universitatis Upsaliensis, 2001), 307–8.

[15]Most of the paintings, including those on the doors of the cabinet, were created by Anton Mozart (1573–1625), who was primarily known as a landscape artist at the time.

[16]In addition to an organ maker, a circle maker, and a stonecutter, special guilds employed by Hainhofer included mirror maker, thimble maker, comb maker, scale maker, sieve maker, and lantern maker. There were as many as ten different kinds of blacksmiths.

[17]Julius von Schlosser, *Die Kunst- und Wunderkammern der Spätrenaissance: ein Beitrag zur Geschichte des Sammelwesens*, (Leipzig: Klinkhardt & Biermann, 1908), 96ff.

[18]Ibid.

[19]Hainhofer's diaries note that Ulrich Baumgartner was depicted as the main craftsman in the painting of the artists, positioned slightly higher than the other artists and holding a compass and protractor in his hands (von Schlosser, op. cit., 114).

[20]After the death of the king in late 1632, it was shipped to Sweden. In 1650, it was moved to Uppsala Castle, and in 1694 Charles XI donated it to the University, where it was placed in the Gustavianum. In 1887, it was moved to the new University Hall and then returned to Museum Gustavianum in connection with its opening in 1997. Johann Fredrik Böttiger, *Philipp Hainhofer und der Kunstschrank Gustav Adolfs in Uppsala* (Stockholm, 1909–10), 48–50.

[21]Daniel Stolcius, who studied at Oxford after fleeing from Bohemia in 1620, produced two of the classic Rosicrucian emblematic texts in *The Pleasure Garden of Chemistry* (1624) and *The Hermetic Garden* (1627) and dedicated *The Hermetic Garden* to Hainhofer, who was described as counselor to the Duke of Pomerania. Hainhofer was recorded as owning a manuscript of one of the manifestoes, the *Fama*, taken from an early draft that must have been in existence before 1613. Ron Heisler, "The Forgotten English Roots of Rosicrucianism," http://www.levity.com/alchemy/h_ros.html, the electronic version of the article published in *The Hermetic Journal*, 1992.

[22]Camillo's theater was actually a memory building representing the order of eternal truth and depicting the various stages of creation. The theater building could accommodate one or two individuals at a time into its interior to see images, figures, and ornaments together with small boxes arranged in various orders and grades, each representing the expanding history of thought. In the first grade were the "seven essential measures" depicted by the "seven known planets" that were the First Causes of creation and on which all things depended. The highest grade of the theater was the seventh level, which was assigned to all the arts, "both noble and vile," as represented by Prometheus, who stole the technology of fire from the gods. Francis A. Yates, *The Art of Memory* (Chicago: The University of Chicago Press, 1966), 130–131.

[23]Frances Yates, *Kabbalah, Magic, and Science: The Cultural Universe of a Sixteenth-Century Jewish Physician* (Cambridge, Mass.: Harvard University Press, 1988), 113.

[24]An example is the Ashmolean Museum at the University of Oxford, which became the first public museum in Great Britain in 1683. It evolved in part out of a cabinet of curiosities that featured pottery and porcelain from China, a Madonna sculpted from feathers, monkey teeth formed into a chain, and a horn from a woman's forehead. Arthur MacGregor, ed., *Tradescant's Rarities: Essays on the Foundation of the Ashmolean Museum 1683, with a Catalogue of the Surviving Early Collections* (Oxford: Clarendon Press, 1983), 15–8.

Curiouser and Curiouser

—Diane Douglas

Executive Director,
Center for Liberal Arts, Bellevue Community College

Diane Douglas is the founding executive director of the Center
for Liberal Arts at Bellevue Community College in metropolitan
Seattle. Douglas served as director of Bellevue Art Museum
between 1991 and 2001. A poet, art critic, curator and educator,
she is actively involved in local and national organizations that
promote the arts, education, and civic engagement. She serves
on the board of the Archie Bray Foundation in Helena, Montana,
and on advisory committees for the Pilchuck Glass School;
Seattle University's master's program in non-profit leadership;
NextBook; and the Center for Craft, Creativity and Design at
the University of North Carolina. Douglas holds an M.A. in
Early American Culture from the University of Delaware and
the Winterthur Program in Early American Culture.

" 'Curiouser and curiouser!' cried Alice (she was so much surprised, that for the moment she quite forgot how to speak good English); 'now I'm opening out like the largest telescope that ever was!' "
—Lewis Carroll, Alice in Wonderland

Curiosity is a noun of great versatility and magic. It defines an object of novelty or beauty made with consummate skill by human hand or by nature. This curiosity sits before you on a table top full-bodied and solid as an apple. But curiosity is also a call, a state of mind and emotion. And, contrastingly, this curiosity is wholly intangible, as mysterious in its origin as in its power to propel us to explore the unknown. Both kinds of curiosity can be found in cabinets of curiosity as a genre of furniture. Both kinds of curiosity were also explicitly discussed in the original rationale and call for proposals developed for this exhibition.

The Cabinets of Curiosity project presents and celebrates wondrous objects. It also examines creativity—the design and folly in assuming challenges, taking risks, solving problems, failing and discovering. How we make art and how we make meaning are intentionally interrelated. I want to explore some of the provocative sites of curiosity and creativity engendered by this project, then push at them and between them—examining the objects themselves, their makers' experiences and our prerogatives as viewer/interpreters.

I also want to look at the parallels between this Cabinets of Curiosity project and the shifting purposes and methods of museums as they collect, display, and interpret art and artifacts. Museums, after all, are nothing more than big cabinets of curiosity. Their modern development, historically and functionally, derives in part from the prototype and popularity of European cabinets of curiosity. Like those antecedents, museums were traditionally built to preserve and display collections of beautiful, precious, exotic, and historically or scientifically significant objects. But their functions today—like the cabinets of curiosity in this exhibition—are much more diverse than originally prescribed. Why is this relationship important? For those of us in the business of exhibiting and writing about art, it's irresistible not to take advantage of the opportunity for self-reflection provided by this meta-analysis. But we hope that the analogy adds value for other viewers too, offering a useful framework for approaching this exhibition and future museum-going experiences.

Drilling Down

Where does curiosity reside in these cabinets of curiosity? Are the cabinets merely the artifact of the creative process of their makers—laden with a curiosity that has been played out in their making, but now is inaccessible to us? Or is it the objects themselves that evoke our curiosity-inviting reverie, inspiring the discovery of something curious about ourselves?

A museum curator, like a physical anthropologist, examines the objects themselves for clues. Close observation of the cabinets' construction reveals different stances in the ways they communicate meaning. While some yield all their secrets to an inspection of their surfaces, most have elements that are hidden away inside drawers or behind doors. It is instructive to explore what information artists choose to reveal and why, and what they choose to conceal.

In their minimalist cabinet of curiosities entitled *Round Guy Meets Square Guy* (Plate 12), Michael Hosaluk and Mitch Ryerson conceal nothing. There is no narrative here. Instead, the curiosity explored is formal: it lies in the artists' attempt to pare down both the cabinet maker's and the wood turner's roles to their bare essentials. In this work, cabinet and curiosity are collapsed in an aesthetic investigation of pure sculpture. In contrast, Miguel Gomez-Ibañez and Joseph Reed have created a cabinet to house wholly hidden

Figure 6
Charles Willson Peale
The Artist in His Museum
1822
Oil on canvas
103 3/4 x 79 7/8 in.
The Pennsylvania Academy of the Fine Arts, Philadelphia.
Gift of Mrs. Sarah Harrison (the Joseph Harrison, Jr. Collection)

curiosities. Their *Vargueño* (Plate 13) is a shell waiting to receive its meaning in the choices and juxtapositions of objects it will store. This cabinet is all about secrets—some of its drawers even have hidden locking mechanisms. Its purpose is to hide and protect its contents for the private consumption of its owner.

Between these two extremes lies Po Shun Leong's *Time Standing Still* (Plate 8). A sculptural portrait of renowned American woodworker Bob Stocksdale, this cabinet combines turned and constructed elements of the artist's making with a clock face and other broken, unfinished and scrap turnings acquired from Stocksdale. This formal homage is openly revealed in the finished cabinet's form. But there is another tribute made and another lineage to be found beyond this obvious one. If you open the drawers located in the sculpture's ribcage, you will find small cross sections of branches—like lab samples—with descriptions of the famous trees in American history from which they derive. These include a tree planted by Johnny Appleseed, a fallen tree at Abraham Lincoln's tomb, a tree associated with Christopher Columbus and a tree from the woods near Henry David Thoreau's Walden Pond. It is as if Po Shun Leong were quietly and humbly acknowledging the deeper soul of American woodworking and revealing his own ecological consciousness in using scraps for his constructed portraits.

We can extract meaning from these cabinets by examining their construction, exploring the relationships between the parts and the whole—that is, between the curiosities and the cabinets. Cabinets of curiosity can be constructed in one of two ways. The first is to start without a frame of reference, to create a container for a collection of discreet objects that will be supplied by another person or at a later date. This is the case with the *Vargueño* cabinet described above; it is an empty vessel waiting to be filled. A second process is to start with a purpose in mind—a question to explore or a story to tell—and then to integrate the cabinet's design with its contents. This alternative was the chosen course for most of the artists in this exhibition. It can be seen in Kurt Nielsen's *Seven Wonders* cabinet (Plate 2), a magical carousel built not only to hold Dan Essig's collection of precious handmade books, but to contextualize it by elaborating on Essig's musings on evolution. Similarly, William Leete's sexy *Holon Form* cabinet (Plate 1) provides a curvaceous, form-fitting case—a body—to display the sensuous biomorphic curiosities—organs—created by his collaborator, ceramist Sam Chung.

These contrasting methods correspond to alternative collecting strategies—pursued either personally or institutionally by museums. The first reflects people who know what they like when they see it and accumulate objects or works of art if and when they are inspired. The objects collected may not come from the same provenance or the same materials. Instead, the common ground, the "glue" for this collection, is the personality and taste of the collector. This situation is akin to the museum—a history or art museum, for example—that collects works representative of its own time, one-by-one, without knowing the cohesive story they will tell retrospectively. The second method is to accumulate objects according to a proactive plan—as in the case of someone who builds a comprehensive collection of 18th-century Japanese swords, for example—in which selections are made more strategically. Art and history museums operate this way when they organize a single artist's retrospective or install thematic exhibitions by gathering artifacts that represent the sequence, details, and ambience of an event they wish to present.

In this exhibition, a deeper look at the relationships between cabinets and curiosities reveals this mixture of motives. Some cabinets demonstrate the psychological impulse to tell a story, to order the facts, and to integrate the elements for us. Others, however, are more open-ended and ambiguous, leaving it up to us to supply the glue that harmonizes the parts into a whole and organizes what we're seeing. In Michelle

Holzapfel's *Story Book* (Plate 10), painstaking efforts are made to document a story and present it in meticulous detail—the story of the construction of this cabinet of curiosities. In a 42-page narrative nested within it, Holzapfel details her cabinet's process of construction, its sources (materials and inspirations), and her relationships to her collaborators. Our role as viewers is to take her story in—visually and verbally—and enjoy the complexity and richness, virtuosity, and craftsmanship of its exposition. The artist has even left room for us to place ourselves within her story by providing a guest book to record viewer comments and responses. Amy Forsyth and Mark Sfiri also explicitly invite our participation in unraveling the story of their *"Figurati . . . "* (*"go figure yourself"*) (Plate 4). But their modus operandi as storytellers is extremely different from Holzapfel's. They provide us an architectural stage set with a series of mysterious objects as protagonists and props. Their cabinet is an invitation to play, to set up the available curiosities in our own sequences and juxtapositions. They allow us to build our own narrative, which is different, in turn, for each viewer/ storyteller and with each juxtaposition/telling. Whereas Holzapfel's cabinet serves a didactic role in educating us about its origins, the Forsyth/Sfiri cabinet is mysterious and evocative, inciting us to explore our own curious pursuits.

The issue of who creates and controls the stories promulgated by these cabinets of curiosity—or by museums in their organization of exhibitions—relates directly to the question of where curiosity resides within them. Artists and curators sometimes use their creative platforms to tell stories and provide insights into realities we can't otherwise know or imagine. But at other times they simply provide raw materials, data for the imagination, and then rely on viewers to construct meaningful narratives of their own. In the first instance, they provide resources to explain curious objects and stimulate critical viewing. In the latter, they evoke curious interpreters as co-creators of stories yet untold.

There are other physical strategies artists use to engender specific relationships between viewers and their work. For example, large objects make you stand back physically and sometimes emotionally, too; small objects pull you in close for careful inspection. In this exhibition, viewer intimacy and involvement are likewise enhanced through the sense of touch. Some cabinets in this exhibition invite touch; others don't. Some demand it as the only way viewers can truly understand what's going on, what they're all about. Christopher Weiland's *Top Secrets* cabinet (Plate 7) looks like a handsome, well-made, but relatively simple box from the outside. It becomes dynamic only when you open its doors. Then you discover the spinning tops made by Weiland but colored by his six-year-old collaborator, Kelly DeLor, and the ways her drawings inspired the sensitive choices of colors, textures, and construction details for his cabinet. The cabinet beckons you to take out the tops, spin them, and enjoy their child-like freshness. As you do, you become part of the artists' collaboration, engaged in the play and delight that stimulated their project from the beginning.

William Leete and Sam Chung's *Holon Form* cabinet creates sexual tension in its simultaneous allure and suggestion of violation with regard to the sense of touch. On the one hand, this cabinet's snowy white surfaces and interiors suggest the environment of a medical exam room or scientific laboratory. Its contents are pure and pristine specimens; they emit the message to keep your hands off. On the other hand, the artists taunt us to touch and rearrange their sensual organic curiosities. Doing so stimulates the not-so-subtle realization that these "specimens" have lost the aura of chastity they had before we picked them up. Touching this cabinet and its curiosities is a transgressive act, akin to experiencing all the pleasures and taboos of encountering and touching a stranger's body.

Risks and Rewards

Art making is risky business by any measure at any time. But this project explicitly ups the ante. It requests that artists collaborate with partners to create their cabinets of curiosity, and it charges them to expand upon the traditional ideas associated with this furniture genre, to give the tradition "a contemporary presence." While there were as many different ways of addressing that challenge as there were participating artists, it is meaningful to look for patterns in the spectrum of work that resulted. What kind of risks were assumed and to what ends?

Most of the artists or artist teams in this exhibition addressed risk as a stretch in technical innovation or the merger of different skill sets to make something greater than an individual could achieve alone. These artists had a goal or vision in mind and the question addressed by their collaboration was: Can we do this or how can we do this? *Givin' Adolf his Props* (Plate 9), a cabinet made by Gideon Hughes and Adolf Volkman, exemplifies this approach. The artists' goal was to recognize the often overlooked, mostly invisible art of pattern makers (like Volkman). Volkman's gears and pulleys inspired Hughes' cabinet, including its recycling of scrap wood slats and its rough and tumble finish. Hughes notes that, "Folk art has [a] simplicity of necessity that I have always admired. Use what you know with what you have on hand to make something." Hughes' earthy sense of aesthetics is completely congruent with Volkman's pragmatic concerns in devising working gears and models. In form, spirit, and function, their collaboration extols the virtues of ingenious craftsmanship and mechanical innovation. A similar purposefulness and harmony of design sensibilities is at work in Michael Brolly's collaboration with John Biggs, Zac Robbins, Chris Coggiano, Tony Delong, and Lynne E. Brolly. Michael Brolly was the project director behind this team's efforts to create an animated "ET"-like creature that interacts with visitors who approach it. They, too, had a clear goal in mind from the collaboration's inception, and while their process involved a lot of improvisation and change along the way, that goal always drove their choices and was successfully realized in the *Cirque de Cabinet* (Plate 5) they produced.

Some artists demonstrated a different creative approach and addressed the issue of risk in a head-on collision, positioning it as the main purpose of their collaboration. Their orientation can be described by an alternative design question: What would happen if . . . ? In their initial proposal for a cabinet entitled *Seeds of Curiosity: Staples of Transformation* (Plate 14), Stephen Hogbin and Jack Larimore articulated this inspiration:

"We have been thinking of the cabinet unfolding physically, formally, and conceptually in an 'organic' process, an interactive revelation in which form and idea are one. Each new folding part [would be] another fragment of the conversation. Folding, hinging, opening like a book that reveals through the action of turning the page. We think the object may be passed back and forth like a conversation. Jack would build a framework to which Stephen would add turned elements to be sent back for further manipulation. At each exchange we would clarify the form and its contents around the organic processes of exchange."

In this collaboration, there was no specific outcome envisioned at the outset. The cabinet was formed from the dialogue between its makers in an evolutionary process of mutual discovery.

Chris Becksvoort began his Shaker Display Cabinet *Threads of Simplicity* (Plate 3) with the intent of building a showcase for authentic Shaker sewing spools and bobbins found in the collection of the Sabbathday Lake Shaker settlement in Maine where he works. But when those original objects were deemed too fragile to be used for this purpose, he altered his plans and, instead, created a meditation on the Shaker spools.

He had them reproduced and, considering them as design elements, posited five alternative ways to display them. He built a new cabinet to chart the path of his curiosity, observation, and response.

Expanding the Lens

Why is it important to document the challenges, risks, and even the paths not taken by the artists in this exhibition? Why not report on their work simply by judging the aesthetic success of the final results? That, after all, is the most traditional means of review exercised by curators who make selections of art to present to the public. They choose works of the greatest merit, defined as the highest aesthetic caliber or serving as a quintessential example of a given era or style. And those criteria are also usually what art critics write about in newspaper reviews, art magazines, and exhibition catalogues.

The problem lies in that traditional evaluation criteria are only partially relevant to this project because of its multiple goals. While one of its aims is to generate fine and unique cabinets of curiosity—which certainly can be judged according to aesthetic merit—another is to stimulate artists' collaborations and experimentation. This second, process-oriented goal cannot at all be judged using traditional qualitative standards. Instead, from the planning stage forward, it required the project curators to make assessments of the experimental journeys that participating artists were proposing to take—even when we had no idea (along with them) what the final results might be or look like.

Like the participating artists, we curators had to take risks. And, as a team, we were not always in immediate agreement and had to negotiate which proposals were the most likely to pan out in fruitful journeys and interesting outcomes. Some of us were more risk-tolerant, some more risk-averse. We talked about what information we had to back up our willingness to go out on a limb—the technical skills of the artists involved, their record of previous work, the originality of their proposals. And against those "data," we weighed our gut feelings about their ability to actualize their plans. In the end, we realized that our role was completely analogous to that of the participating artists. We were there to create a big cabinet of curiosities from their collective work, where every one of their projects became a curiosity within the virtual cabinet or curatorial frame of our design.

We also realized that viewer/interpreters of this exhibition would have to wrestle with the same mix of value judgments. They would have to decide for themselves how to evaluate success under these circumstances—when they liked the results, when their curiosity was sated, or perhaps when they felt artists took big risks and pulled them off. In order to facilitate those judgments, we felt we had to document the artists' creative paths. As curators, we wanted to provide viewers access to the same records of their creative ups and downs as we had. At the same time, we also questioned our obligations to artists given the unorthodoxy of the competition. We felt ambivalent in cases where artists had completed cabinets that were significantly different and sometimes aesthetically disappointing given their initial proposals, yet they had taken chances and finished their collaborations in good faith. We wondered what you, viewers and readers, would think of us if we admitted those cabinets to the exhibition. Would you think we'd fallen down on the job—not picking works of the highest caliber by the traditional standards? Or could we explain our motives and engage you in the process of weighing alternatives and making judgments, too, so that we'd all end up as mutual explorers on the same curious journey? Could we transform the nature of your expectations and the nature of the exhibition from a showcase into a laboratory?

In the end, not only the organization of the project but the art itself set the tone. The cabinets in this exhibition are intrinsically, inescapably eclectic. Like their historical antecedents, they accommodate tangible and intangible curiosities. They house objects whose significance may lie in their artistic, scientific, or historical meanings. This innate complexity reinforced our reluctance to evaluate them on the basis of traditional aesthetics alone. We are all sometimes bewildered by contemporary art when our expectations don't coincide with the intent or effect of the works we encounter. As pleasure seekers we can be put off when we experience ugly, raw, politically charged, ambiguous or tough art. As viewers who desire conceptual challenge, we may find beautiful objects vapid if that's all they have to offer. In this exhibition and many others, the meaning and value of what you find depends upon what you seek and, as seekers, we all have different expectations, different curiosities.

Transformation

Chris Becksvoort takes Shaker sewing spools out of their historical and functional context and forces us to reconsider them in a new light. By reproducing them, hanging them end-to-end and placing them individually on a pedestal, Becksvoort asserts their status as elements of sculpture. He makes us realize that these seemingly humble objects are also formally wonderful, technically adroit, and beautiful. He encourages their appreciation as art. A corollary of this process is found in the previously discussed cabinets, *Holon Form* and *"Figurati . . . " ("go figure yourself")*. Here small abstract sculptures morph into actors, building parts and body parts. They are infused with meaning as we align and realign them within frames of reference suggested by their creators.

This ability to make us see things in new ways—to make the strange familiar and the familiar strange—is one of art's most powerful and provocative functions. It is accomplished through artists' observations, analyses, and experiments—processes also associated with the work of scientists. But whereas scientific research aims to explain the unknown, artists reaffirm the majesty of the unknown, even as they mine and map its secrets. In his insightful essay, "The Wonder of it All: Contemporary Cabinets of Curiosity," Joseph Goldyne discusses these disciplinary affinities and differences:

"Art conceals as much as it exposes. It nourishes the mind and emotions not by solving problems, but by stimulating wonder. To do so, employing the magnificently rich traditions of science, it must often employ the equipment and forms characteristic of the scientific traditions of inquiry, but it must employ them differently than for the purposes to which they were originally devoted."

Science's aim to explicate the unknown and art's power to reinforce mystery are juxtaposed in cabinets of curiosity which have always accommodated artifacts from both realms. In presenting their miscellaneous wonders side by side, these cabinets blur the distinction between objects collected because of their scientific merit, their aesthetic interest, and their emotional meanings. Instead, all of these appeals are celebrated together and given equal valence. In his book, *Mr. Wilson's Cabinet of Wonder: Pronged Ants, Horned Humans, Mice on Toast, and Other Marvels of Jurassic Technology*, Lawrence Weschler describes what happens as viewers encounter this promiscuous mixing of values:

"The visitor . . . continually finds himself shimmering between wondering at the marvels of nature and wondering whether any of this could possibly be true. And it's that very shimmer, the capacity for such delicious confusion that may constitute the most blessedly wonderful thing about being human."

Encountering mystery, taking risks, making sense, and making connections—these are the tasks we face as viewers/interpreters of art and of life. These cabinets of curiosity offer rewarding journeys of discovery, and the curiouser we are, the more our attentiveness will be rewarded: "Now I'm opening out like the largest telescope that ever was"—seeing things, old and new, in a new light, with equal parts understanding and wonder.

A Relationship with Legs:

Wood Turning and Furniture Making in Cabinets of Curiosities

—Rick Mastelli

Editor, photographer, videographer,
and principal at Image & Word

Rick Mastelli has been a craft editor, photographer, and writer
since 1979. He worked on *Fine Woodworking* magazine in the
black-and-white years, then created Taunton's Video Workshop
series. He has produced, directed, and edited how-to video-
tapes on woodworking, homebuilding, and the fiber arts,
including several award winners. Since establishing Image &
Word, a publishing services partnership, he has contributed
to books on woodworking, basketry, gardening, cooking,
homebuilding, and American cultural history. From 1993 to
1997, he edited and produced *American Woodturner*, the
journal of the American Association of Woodturners. From
1996 to 2001, he was special advisor to The Furniture Society,
editing its newsletter and co-editing the *Furniture Studio*
books.

Among the several goals of this ambitious exhibition is to encourage collaboration between wood turners and furniture makers. These days, most wood turners don't make furniture, and many furniture makers have mixed feelings about the lathe. It's a captivating tool, with what may be unlimited potential, and that alone can be intimidating. It also seems self-contained, inward-looking, its function epitomized in the production of the artful vessel. The lathe commands a unique relationship with woodworkers: those who love it usually love it for its ability to create finished objects quickly, not for its efficiencies or stylistic repertoire in fashioning furniture parts.

Wood turning is the only woodworking process in which a machine moves the wood past a handtool. It demands different skills, a different sensibility, and, with the potential for a massive piece of work to fly off the lathe and become a missile, more respect than other woodworking activities.[1] Furniture making involves diverse preparatory and constructive procedures. Wood turning tends to funnel your attention on the moment at hand. It calls for dynamic interaction, engaging the whole body, like a dance.[2] Chance—discovering and working with the natural features of the material and balancing machined precision with wood's organic irregularity—plays a larger role in the turner's (certainly in the art vessel maker's) creativity than it does in the furniture maker's.[3]

Of course there are tendencies to the contrary. James Krenov's influential approach to cabinetmaking emphasizes "listening" to the wood.[4] And wood turning as practiced by technical virtuosos such as Ray Allen or Michael Shuler entails planning and procedures no less complex than those involved in producing a complicated piece of furniture.[5] But in the main, woodworkers today are drawn to turning for its immediacy and to furniture making for the more gradual satisfactions that come from design and construction.

This division was not always so. Before the middle of the 19th century, furniture makers, or joiners, commonly relied on the lathe in their work. Saws and planes were used to size and smooth boards and panels; lathes were used to shape legs and stretchers. In addition to being an extremely efficient tool for making chair, table, and cabinet-stand parts, the lathe was exploited for its repertoire of decorative effects. Furniture styles of the 16th and 17th centuries were dependent on lathe-turned features. Beads, coves, ogees, and fillets trace back to elements in classical architecture, and they appear not only in the structural components of furniture but as applied decoration. (*See Figure 7, Vargueño from Gomez-Ibañez proposal.*)

In his 1997 World Turning Conference presentation, "Turning and Contemporary Studio Furniture: An Uneasy Relationship," Edward S. Cooke, Jr., chronicles the evolution of wood turning and its relation to furniture making from what might be called the lathe's golden age through the end of the 20th century.[6] Even before the Industrial Revolution, turning began to develop as a specialty, and some furniture makers purchased turned parts from wood turners rather than make their own. Industrialization increased the separateness of the trades, as production from replicating lathes dominated the marketplace and encroached upon the work of the specialty turner. By the end of the 19th century, turned elements and decorations in furniture were associated with mechanized, soulless production, debased both technically and aesthetically.

Cabinetmaking, invigorated by the Arts and Crafts Movement, had a different encounter with mechanization. As tastes eschewed turned furniture forms, high-quality wood craftsmanship became associated with rectilinear shapes and simple, "honest" surfaces, as in the so-called Mission style (notwithstanding that another machine, the table saw, was responsible for the style's proliferation). In any

Figure 7
Artist unknown
Vargueño
17th century
Wood, with gilded iron mounts; arcaded stand with shell pulls.
Locked; one outer key; one key to cupboards.
Top: 63 1/2 x 104 x 42 cm., Base: 81 x 85 x 54 cm.
The Hispanic Society of America, New York

event, Modernism in the early 20th century, championing new materials and new technologies, marginalized traditional cabinetmaking as well.

By the time furniture tastes had rediscovered an appreciation for natural materials and conventional structures (in the form of Scandinavian Modernism introduced to this country in 1939), both trades were barely surviving. But with the decline of woodworking as a trade came a vigorous interest in it as a hobby. Woodworking attracted blue-collar and white-collar males (mainly), as an opportunity to exercise design sensibilities, manual skills, and control over the whole of the process of making things, from raw material to finished product. Relatively autonomous, the lathe became the most popular recreational woodworking tool. But trail-blazing studio furniture makers such as Wharton Esherick, George Nakashima, and Sam Maloof did not embrace the lathe the way they embraced other tools. Those who were attracted to the lathe, like Bob Stocksdale and Art Carpenter, used it to turn bowls and treen rather than furniture parts.

Studio furniture making and wood turning advanced through the subsequent decades separately, along different lines. Furniture making became more technically sophisticated, as traditional methodologies were rediscovered and improved upon. Wood turning, nearly severed from its past glories, explored new territories, as turners first celebrated wood figure as a decorative element in bowl turning, then pushed past the utilitarian boundaries of the vessel and convened at symposiums to share their prodigious innovations. Eventually old ways of turning wood (hollowing with hook tools, for instance, or practicing the efficiencies of the pole lathe) were reassimilated. Now, furniture makers and wood turners have each, in their own ways, mastered their craft's technical demands and are exploring conceptual issues in their work. Organizations like the Wood Turning Center and the Furniture Society offer conferences, exhibitions, and publications to facilitate interchange, promote growth, and chronicle developments.

Yet, as Cooke notes, there is a "paucity of furniture with lathe-based work." Looking back over the evolving relationships between the two fields, he asks the question, "Is there a possibility for reconciliation between turning and studio furniture making?"[7] In some ways, *Cabinets of Curiosities* is an attempt to answer that question positively. Cooke himself postulates three different directions in which this question might lead. Each direction is indeed represented in this show.

The first is a revival of the integration that furniture making and wood turning enjoyed of yore. *Vargueño* (Plate 13), built by Miguel Gomez-Ibañez, could hardly be a clearer representation of this direction. Based on a design from sixteenth-century Spain, the vargueño features both traditional cabinetmaking and wood turning in forms designed to complement one another. A large case, plain and simple when closed, sits atop an ornate base. The case is dovetailed, with a flat fall-front panel and an unmolded, unraised frame-and-panel back; the joinery calls no attention to itself. Originally, the vargueño, was used to store and transport valuable objects. It included carrying handles at the sides, reinforcing ironwork at the corners, and prominent hinges, clasp, and lock, all often intricately detailed, as Spanish ironwork represented the height of the craft at the time. Gomez-Ibañez has chosen to keep his case austere on the outside, to contrast more effectively with the lively interior, a surprising facade of colorful drawer fronts, designed and painted by Joseph W. Reed, each in a different floral subject corresponding to a letter of the alphabet.

The base is also a simplified version of what in the original might have included a dozen or more spindle turnings composing two post-and-rail leg structures connected across the middle by a frame-and-spindle trestle. Here, such a trestle has been replaced by plain stretchers at the top and bottom of the base, which opens the middle of the base and concentrates the decorative detailing in the leg assemblies. The turnings are spiral fluted on the lower sections and carved into bines above. The contrast between the refined fluting and the more primitive spiral carving generates an appealing energy that is entirely in keeping with the baroque spirit of the original design.

Gomez-Ibañez says he enjoyed most developing the spiral turnings.[8] In his research, comparing numerous vargueños, he noted that the spiral leg was common, varying widely in proportions and detailing. He had never made a spiral turning before, so he practiced. He tried a router setup, which worked but produced results that were too regular. Close handwork proved to be the most satisfying procedure. He came to appreciate the vinelike character of the spirals, recognizing their appropriateness to the vegetal theme of the piece. The combination of lathework and handwork, along with traditional cabinetmaking techniques, produced a composition that breathes new life into an archaic format. Gomez-Ibañez, like many studio furniture makers, finds inspiration in vintage furniture forms. Depending on the style, wood turning, not a primary interest, is more or less a part of the work.

Another piece in this exhibition that incorporates traditionally turned elements is *Seven Wonders* (Plate 2), built by Kurt Nielsen to house the handmade books of Daniel Essig. The globe (both outer and inner), the supporting columns, and the finial are turned, while the cabinet shell is glued up from thin, flexible plies of wood on a cylindrical form. Like many contemporary furniture makers, Nielsen has no particular affinity for the lathe. He admits to avoiding it when he can: "Procedurewise, the lathe scares me," he says in his response to the exhibition questionnaire, although "this piece has pulled me out of my concept of turning as a step in furniture making into thinking of it as a procedure unto itself."

The turnings in this piece are not ancillary but central to its theme and its design. The globe is symbolic of the worldly universality of the books the cabinet contains. The cabinet itself—round, suspended on an axis, and (as according to myth) resting on the back of a turtle—represents the world, too. The interior revolves to display a series of compartments, each one revealing the stages of evolution of a different life form. This is the world captured and conveyed through the amber of craft.

In its design integration of wood turning with studio furniture making, *Seven Wonders* points toward the second direction for reconciliation between the two, that is, the direction taken by those who effect a give-and-take between the two idioms, advancing both in the process. Cooke refers to the example of Mark Sfirri, whom I will talk about in a later context. Christopher Weiland, whose *Top Secrets* (Plate 7) features turned elements as well as contents (colorfully decorated by Kelly Delor), first synthesized furniture and turned forms in 1984.[9] Weiland's strategies for producing a balanced, unified design include understating the turned features and separating them from rectilinear elements with marginal space that adds accenting shadow detail. He also employs turnings functionally, in exposed joinery, and in moving or adjustable components. Turned elements are thus given purpose as well as an integral visual appeal. These strategies are evident in *Top Secrets*: The doors are hinged on turned cylinders, which are partially recessed into the cabinet's top and bottom rails. The spindles of the tops that the cabinet contains, finished in the same contrasting color as the hinge cylinders, also protrude from the front of the cabinet, through an accentuating space between the doors. These turned elements are thus visually pronounced when the cabinet is closed and speak to each other. By the functioning of the hinge, the tops are made accessible. To release them, you manipulate another turned process, pivoting the dowels that hold the tops in place.

Another approach in this second direction to integrating wood turning and furniture making emanates from the work of Stephen Hogbin. Hogbin's influence is acknowledged by a number of people in this show (including William Leete, Michael Brolly, Michael Hosaluk, and Mark Sfirri), and *Seeds of Curiosity: Staples of Transformation* (Plate 14), the piece he created in collaboration with Jack Larimore for this show, evidences an understated relation to the approach he spawned. Trained as an industrial designer in the 1960s, Hogbin was attracted to the lathe because it enabled him "to develop and fabricate a number of ideas in rapid succession. . . . The dominant feature of a lathe-turned plate is its circular outline. Cutting into that circle seemed the most likely way of developing new forms."[10] As Hogbin proceeded to cut and reassemble plates and other turned forms, he discovered and developed a seemingly endless range of possibilities, which he came to call "fragmentals," that have utilitarian, decorative, architectural, and sculptural applications, including, of course, in furniture.

The work in this show that calls Hogbin's fragmentals most to mind is William Leete's turnings in *Holon Form* (Plate 1). The ceramic forms that accompany this piece, by collaborator Sam Chung, have a similar flavor, though the process for producing them does not involve the lathe. As the proposal for this piece indicated, "the main theme is to express the process of collaboration through the relationship of two separate sets of forms coming together and creating a third set." Fulfilling that theme, "the concept of duality or yin and yang or male and female" is apparent, as well as larger surfaces coming from smaller ones and different forms joining, all evidencing how the whole is "made up of the relationships of parts through multiple levels of existence." The makers refer to the concept of "holons" in the writings of philosopher Ken Wilber: whole/parts, of which everything can be understood to consist. It is interesting to note that while Leete and Chung indicate they "deliberately chose shapes that suggest budding plant and animal forms," the process Leete employed—two faceplate turnings, cut in half, carved, and reassembled in a new arrangement—is classic fragmental turning. Hogbin's approach not only lends itself to the generative design of this piece but embodies the interactivity between process and product that is the theme of *Holon Form*. This dynamic give-and-take continues with the viewers' interactivity, invited as they are to organize and rearrange the parts of the piece indefinitely. We jurors were captivated by the work, discovering how the larger pieces could serve as nests for the smaller and fascinated by how groupings could take on familial relationships. Among the works that serve the mission of this show "to advance the understanding of design, materials, techniques, and their traditions," this one, which so intrigues and engages the viewer, goes especially far.

Michael Brolly also integrates wood turning with furniture making by using the lathe as a design, not just a production, tool; he creates sculpture rooted in both idioms.[11] His early work was not guided by conventional methodologies but rather by idiosyncratic reinvention. He used the lathe along with other tools in his own ways, to sculpt his peculiar imaginative forms. By the time Brolly encountered Hogbin's explorations (in 1981 through the *Turned Objects Show*), there was little danger that the influence, though profound, would blunt the artist's edge. "Since I went to art school," Brolly writes in response to the questionnaire for this exhibition, "copying was out." Where Hogbin has tended to evidence a clear connection to the geometry of the original forms and the processes that transform them, Brolly often disguises the geometric connections by giving character and personality to the forms. In *Cirque de Cabinet* (Plate 5), Brolly begins with relatively simple turnings to create the carcase of his cabinet/creature, as well as its head and connecting elements. Then he cuts and reconfigures the parts and (thanks to his several collaborators, Christopher Coggiano, Lynn E. Brolly, Anthony DeLong, Zachery Robbins, and John Biggs) adds color, movement, a blown-glass belly, and a pair of engaging eyes. Interactivity takes a surprising turn in this piece, as you discover that the creature almost sentiently responds to your own movements. The ambiguity (is this creature friendly, nurturing a brood of amusing kin, or voracious, stocking its larder with who knows what next?) is typical of Brolly's work. He likes to keep us guessing, and using the lathe in surprising ways is among his effective means.

The third direction toward reconciliation between wood turning and furniture making is collaboration between practitioners of the two. Collaboration has been a powerful force in advancing contemporary wood turning. As art and craft writer Suzanne Ramljak points out, wood turning's embrace of collaboration can be traced to the attitude wood turners have toward their material. The organic irregularity of wood is valued, incorporated, relied upon. Encountered as it is on the lathe by chance and accepted or shaped in a dynamic, interactive relationship, the unique properties of wood (its color, grain, figure, defects) multiply wood turning's opportunities for creativity and expressiveness. This is especially valuable at the lathe, where the machine's capacity for mechanical perfection threatens to overwhelm the work. Ramljak recognizes how, by including the name of the material when signing their own name to the work, that is, in their "open acknowledgement of nature as a creative partner," wood turners promulgate a certain critique of individualism.[12]

Perhaps as a natural outgrowth of wood turning's balance of the individual among multiple sources of creativity, collaboration between individual wood turners is familiar, one of the important ways the field works. A short list of effective collaborative efforts would include the work of Mark Sfirri and Michael Hosaluk, the Wood Turning Center's International Turning Exchange, the Saskatoon (a.k.a. Emma Lake) Conferences, the annual American Association of Woodturners Chapter Collaborative Challenges, the sculptural orchestrations that Steve Loar creates from the leavings of his colleagues (an approach also exercised by Po Shun Leong, who uses the broken bowls and scraps of Bob Stocksdale, in *Time Standing Still* (Plate 8)) and, of course, this very show, which was initiated by the Wood Turning Center. Furniture making, too, has known collaboration; the Emma Lake Conferences encompass both endeavors, and the Surface Design sessions at The Furniture Society conferences generate vigorous collaborative activities.[13] Notably, both these venues have achieved the vitality they have in large part through the initiative and ongoing efforts of Michael Hosaluk, who, though he began as a furniture maker, became a wood turner for the predictable reason that turning is more immediate, more responsive—the same qualities that characterize the collaborative work he has championed. Hosaluk is billed as the "round guy" paired with "square guy" Mitch Ryerson in their proposal for this show: "A round guy and a square guy have agreed to jump off two cliffs at the same time so they can meet at the bottom." The result, *Round Guy Meets Square Guy* (Plate 12), is a playful, rudimentary interpretation of the relationship between the two fields.

Collaboration is evidently contagious, as it has spread in this show well beyond the called-for interaction between wood turners and furniture makers. Included are collaborative contributions from book makers, painters, a ceramist, a glass blower, a patternmaker, a photographer, an animitronicist, and a child, not to mention the training among participants in industrial design, architecture, mechanical engineering, and literature (Italian as well as English).

But to see how well wood turning and furniture making may fair through collaboration, you couldn't do better than to consider *"Figurati . . . "* (*"go figure yourself"*) (Plate 4) by architecture teacher and furniture maker Amy Forsyth, and turner and furniture maker Mark Sfirri. As has been noted, Sfirri is a seasoned collaborator. His teaming up with Forsyth here for the first time has provided more than interesting results; the finished work serves as a display stand for Forsyth's record of the piece's development, including her colorful sketches and select email exchanges between the two makers. Blank pages at the end of the book are offered for viewers to record their interactions with the piece while it is on exhibition, extending the collaboration, if you will.

The piece began auspiciously in the proposal stage, referencing quotes from Walter Benjamin ("A novel is not a place one passes through; it is a place one inhabits") and Gaston Bachelard ("Sometimes a lovingly fashioned cabinet has interior perspectives that change constantly as a result of day dream. We open it and discover that it is a dwelling place, that a house has hidden in it."). The developmental drawings suggest architectural space (a checkered floor, walls and columns, a raftered roof, anterooms) in which figures find themselves. They relate variously to the built environment, to movable props (architectural elements that serve as furniture within the furniture/architectural space), and to each other. Thus, several media are evoked: the novel, the theater, the game board, the doll house, the dream. Furniture making is here exercised as small-scale, gestural architecture, while wood turning, itself the more performance-oriented craft, yields the figures to occupy and animate the symbolic space. In its abstract, surreal quality, the finished piece calls to mind the film *Last Year at Marienbad* by Alain Robbe-Grillet and Alain Resnais. There, too, evocative architecture, statuesque figures, and a plot that plays like a convoluted chess game come together into a whole that provokes rumination.

Sfirri's fascinating multi-axis turnings are not only showcased in this work, but the legs that support the case represent his latest and perhaps best application of the technique, especially because they are so well integrated. Sfirri began exploring the possibilities of multi-axis work in 1976 in a series of faceplate-turned trays, which he re-turned to create an offset border, and then in sculpting panels for a frame-and-panel chest. His multi-axis spindle work began in 1992, with his candlestick series; the figures that populate the interior of *"Figurati . . . "* (*"go figure yourself"*) most resemble these forms, though they are more relaxed. In 1993, he first applied these wonky shapes to table legs (the same year he created "Rejects from the Baseball Bat Factory"). His first multi-axis freestanding figurative sculptures, where symmetrical and asymmetrical offset shapes take on anatomical reference, appeared in 1997. In *"Figurati . . . "* (*"go figure yourself"*), these figurative sculptures are made to serve as legs, reminiscent of Greek caryatids (or, if you see them as more masculine, atlantes; Sfirri regards them as androgynous, and there is no Greek term for that). Abstracted as they are and with their posture conforming to a familiar S-curve, they also harken back to cabriole legs before Hogarth celebrated them for their "line of beauty." In fact, early cabrioles were articulated with a similar angular transition, as in the leg of a goat, after which the form was named (from the Italian *capriola*, meaning "goat's leap").[14] Sfirri, no afficionado of tradition per se, has nevertheless brought together two powerful traditional forms—caryatid and cabriole—to create a compelling amalgam. A new, fully lathe-turned form, it is also a fully functional furniture component. The detailing is quite sophisticated, as the two front legs are not identical but bilaterally symmetrical. And their placement, set forward from the edge of the frame they support, observes the positioning of classical columns in their relation to the supported entablature. Sfirri admits that this is more conservative work than he usually does, and perhaps working in accord with the architectural background that Forsyth brings to this collaboration is responsible for that. Whatever the reason, the leg turnings are well integrated not only structurally but thematically, providing an appropriate base for the mobile multi-axis figures that populate the cabinet above.

As Forsyth says in response to the show's questionnaire, "In both disciplines [wood turning and furniture making], I am less interested in pieces that are focused only upon themselves and more interested in the ways in which they work together to create an idea or an environment. This is why I feel *Cabinets of Curiosities* is such an interesting project—juxtaposing the two disciplines creates a conversation held within the piece." Indeed, as one of the goals of *Cabinets of Curiosities* is to bring wood turning more closely together with studio furniture making, the Forsyth/Sfirri approach goes furthest, revisiting familiar territories as well as exploring new ones.

[1] A typical relationship to the lathe is captured in Kurt Nielsen's response to this exhibition questionnaire's background question: "My original attraction was the lathe because of its immediacy. But, alas, after multiple, unintentional propulsion experiments and many near misses and a few lacerations, my instructor thought I might be better off with traditional woodworking skills and hand cut joinery."

[2] Compare Amy Forsyth's response to the questionnaire's request for a comparison of the two activities: "To me, turning seems to be some sort of 'zen-like' thing—you practice for years and finally you have this incredible facility and can crank out beautiful things one after another. Cabinetmaking requires more planning ahead of time—it's much less immediate.…[Wood turning appears to be a] kind of fast performance art."

[3] For more on the dialogue between woodturning's machined precision and organic irregularity, see Suzanne Ramljak in "As the World Turns: Woodturning in an Expanded Context," *Turning Wood into Art: The Jane and Arthur Mason Collection*, (New York: Abrams, 2000). Also see David Ellsworth, "Exploring the Dimensions of Green and Distressed Wood," Turning Points (Summer 2000)

[4] James Krenov, *The Fine Art of Cabinetmaking* (Scarborough, Ontario: Van Nostrand Reignhold, 1977), Chapter 1.

[5] See Ray Allen, "Ray Allen's Segmented Turnings" *American Woodturner* March 1993, pp. 2–8; and Michael Shuler, "Segmented Turning," *Fine Woodworking* #76 (May 1989), pp. 72–75.

[6] I rely on Cooke's presentation, published in *Papers from the 1997 World Turning Conference* (Philadelphia: Wood Turning Center, 2000), not only in summarizing the history of the evolving relationship between the two crafts but in organizing the ways to see how the relationship plays out in several of the "Cabinets of Curiosities." For a more detailed view of the history of the crafts, particularly that of contemporary wood turning in North America, see Cooke's "Turning Wood in America," *Expressions in Wood: Masterworks fom the Wornick Collection* (Oakland: Oakland Museum of California, 1996) and "From Manual Training to Freewheeling Craft: The Transformation of Wood Turning, 1900–76," *Wood Turning in North America Since 1930* (New Haven: Wood Turning Center and Yale University Art Gallery, 2001).

[7] Another view of this situation is found in Mark Sfirri's response to the "Cabinets of Curiosities" questionnaire regarding recent developments in the two fields: "There is a common notion that the turning field is about vessels and to a large extent that's true, but there are also many people who incorporate turned elements into furniture. At the Furniture Society conference in Tempe, AZ, two years ago, I gave a talk called 'Turning in Furniture.' In it I showed the work of nearly fifty contemporary makers who use lathe-turned work in their furniture. Additionally, it was combined in fifteen different ways. I think that collaborative conferences like the Emma Lake conferences in Saskatchewan have played a big part in bringing turners and furniture makers together. Curiously, turning is not a part of any of the major furniture programs in the country. I find it puzzling to still be the case. Turning is a big part of the work produced in the wood medium today, and yet it isn't integrated into wood programs. Its lot seems to be reserved for workshops and summer programs."

[8] For insights into each maker's relation to the work in this exhibition, I have used the notes they provided, email exchanges with them, and interviews, mostly conducted by phone in December 2002.

[9] See Christopher Weiland, *Integrating Lathe-Turned Components in Furniture*, Fine Woodworking #96 (October 1992).

[10] Stephen Hogbin, *Turning Full Circle*, Fine Woodworking #21, p. 56 (March 1980). Also see Hogbin, Wood Turning: *The Purpose of the Object* (Sydney, Australia: John Ferguson, 1980).

[11] In addition to notes provided with this exhibition piece and conversations with the artist, I have consulted the catalog to Brolly's 2002 show, *Michael Brolly: Cradle to Cradle* (Erie, Pennsylvania: Erie Art Museum, 2002), which includes a retrospective look at his work since 1973, an artist's statement, and Glenn Adamson's, "Enfant Terrible: The Work of Michael Brolly."

[12] Ramljak, *op. cit.*, p. 22 ff.

[13] Discussions of collaboration have become extensive. Following is a select list of publications: Mark Sfirri, "Collaborative Work: Its Context and Recent Beginnings" (followed by related articles by Michael Hosaluk, Richard, Raffan, Giles Gilson, and Del Stubbs), *American Woodturner*, December 1993; Mark Sfirri and Michael Hosaluk, "Collaboration in Wood Turning 1986 to Present," *Papers from the 1997 World Turning Conference* (Philadelphia: Wood Turning Center, 2000); Steve Loar, "A Crucible of Invention," *The Craft Factor*, Fall 1998; Hayley Smith, "Hayley Smith/Todd Hoyer Collaboration," *Turning Points* (Winter/Spring 1999); Michael Hosaluk, "Emma Lake: Looking Back and Looking Forward," *Turning Points* (Winter 2001)

[14] See Oscar P. Fitzgerald, Four Centuries of American Furniture (Radnor, Pennsylvania: Wallace-Homestead, 1995), pp. 36–37.

Mind-blowers

—Tom Loeser

Professor of Art, University of Wisconsin-Madison

Tom Loeser, a furnituremaker/educator, has been head of the
wood/furniture program at the University of Wisconsin-
Madison since 1991. He holds a BFA from Boston University's
Program in Artisanry and an MFA from the University of
Massachusetts-North Dartmouth. He has also taught at Rhode
Island School of Design and California College of Arts and
Crafts. His artwork has been included in over 150 national and
international exhibitions since 1981. He is represented in the
collections of several museums and universities including the
Museums of Fine Arts in Boston and Houston, The Renwick
Gallery, The Cooper Hewitt Museum, The Yale University Art
Gallery, The Milwaukee Museum of Art and the Brooklyn
Museum.

Lawrence Weschler, in his 1995 book *Mr. Wilson's Cabinet of Wonder,* describes the late 16th- and early 17th-century cabinets of curiosity as collections of wondrous objects, and in themselves objects that induced wonder in the viewer:

"The point is that for a good century and a half after the discovery of the Americas, *Europe's mind was blown.* That was the animating spirit behind, and the enduring significance of, the profusion of *Wunderkammern.* . . . It was how the palpable reality of such artifacts so vastly expanded the territory of the now readily conceivable. . . . Obviously the mathematical and navigational sophistication necessary for Columbus to have been able to mount an expedition to America—and the make it back, and not once, but four times! —was of a considerable level, and was indicative of a steadily rising curve of such certain positive knowledge (the earth wasn't flat, and there clearly weren't sea monsters lurking along its edge to swallow up any stray doubters). But the stuff he found in America, and the stuff he brought back, was so strange and so new as to seem to sanction belief in all manner of wondrous prospects and phantasms for years thereafter."[1]

Cabinets of curiosities remain an ongoing subject for exploration. Yet the modern revisiting of this topic can never have the same meaning as the cabinets described above by Weschler. The context has changed too much over the intervening 300 years. The world is made smaller by more information moving more quickly to more places. In addition, science offers many more rational explanations of the universe around us. It is harder to find the appropriately mind-blowing artifacts in today's world. Where does that boundary that generates curiosity and provokes wonder exist today?

Despite the challenge of a changed context, a slow but steady stream of shows deal with the topic. David Wilson's Museum of Jurassic Technology (the primary subject of Weschler's book) in Los Angeles plays on the tradition of cabinets of curiosity, and on museums and collecting in general. To the museum's great credit, its exhibits, hovering ambiguously between fact and fiction, are so elusive that Weschler can never quite finally determine if the place is for real or not, even when he does exhaustive "scientific" checks of data bases and makes phone calls to verify the veracity of the artifacts.

Damian Hirst, the poster-child for the current generation of young British artists, makes work that riffs on aspects of the wunderkammern. His trademark steel and glass vitrines are empty spaces (cabinets) in which he displays "mind-blowing" artifacts. The most well known is *The Physical Impossibility of Death in the Mind of Someone Living,* the 1991 signature piece from the *Sensation* exhibition which features a full-size tiger shark floating in a 5 percent formaldehyde solution in a vitrine. Where the historical cabinets often made a fetish of seeking out extraordinary miniature achievements, Hirst super-sizes his 20th-century artifact.

In another Hirst formaldehyde vitrine piece, *Some Comfort Gained from the Acceptance of the Inherent Lies in Everything,* he slices up many cross-sections of two cows and presents them as a fully realized and quite shocking three-dimensional version of a CAT-scan. Perhaps medical imaging, which exists at the boundaries of our newest scientific achievements, and allows us to see and understand what we have never been able to see before, is an appropriate mind-blowing "artifact" of wonder for our times.

In *No Feelings* from 1989, Hirst filled every space on every shelf of a wall cabinet with prescription drugs of every shape size and color. Aside from the sheer physical beauty of the "artifacts," here again he has successfully located a territory appropriate to the wunderkammern concept. The absurdly large inventory of pharmaceutical artifacts represents the edge of scientific knowledge. For most of us non-scientists, the pills remain incomprehensible magical devices.

On a more broad-based and society-wide level, it is hard to ignore the huge role EBay plays in making collecting a major pastime in contemporary culture. Artifacts for everyone's personal cabinets of curiosity are just a web-search away.

So if a contemporary cabinet of curiosity is a different animal, how will a group of highly skilled and creative makers, whose work is often functional, bring a 21st-century sense of wonder and curiosity into the objects for this show? In addition to this commentary on the exhibit's overall aspects, detailed explorations of selected pieces will examine that question later in this essay.

More often than not, when cabinetmakers build a cabinet, they are constructing an "unfinished" object that defines and contains an interior volume. That volume is then turned over to the purchaser/user for their discretionary use. The user has a large say in defining the final role and meaning of the piece. The opportunity to build a cabinet of curiosity creates a fundamentally different role for the maker. In this case, the maker is offered the chance to "complete" the work by filling the cabinet literally through the installation of specific objects, or figuratively through the storytelling aspects of the work.

The diversity and inventiveness of the work generated for this show make it impossible to generalize accurately about all of them. However, overall the pieces certainly incorporate an increased interest in narrative, and a reduced role for function. Where did function go? Much of what would usually be the "useful" space in these cabinets is filled with various story-telling devices and objects of wonder. The question of how the cabinets are to be used has been both asked and answered.

Collaboration is another important aspect of this show and is crucial to many of these pieces. Both the theme of the show and its structure, with its invitation to submit proposals, served as an impetus for makers to share ideas and expertise. The reward is that we get to see pieces that probably would not have come out of these makers' studios, in this form, if they were working by themselves.

Amy Forsyth and Mark Sfirri's collaboration *"Figurati . . . "* (*"go figure yourself"*) (Plate 4) looks like a piece of furniture. It has a lower section built in a traditional table format, using four beautiful offset turnings for the legs. The table supports a house-like structure. Although there are two small drawers, the piece has no functional qualities in the traditional sense. The drawers hold various turned or carved shapes in custom fitted spaces. These non-specific and non-identifiable chess-like pieces are only part of a parts inventory that includes some identifiable images such as books, a ladder, a slug, a turtle shell, a colonnade, and a small portable wall that incorporates a window with a severe case of shrinking perspective. Various references to two-dimensional perspective conventions and the use of shifting vanishing points make the interior spaces elusive and adaptable. The viewer is invited to move parts around, inserting them in different places within the house, or putting some parts away, allowing for a constantly shifting self-created dialogue.

One side of the roof serves as a lectern, supporting a partly filled journal which contains source material for the piece. It includes architectural drawings, written and drawn notes from travels as well as documentation of the collaboration, including letters between Forsyth and Sfirri, as well as the various design sketches for the piece. The imagery shows an ongoing interest in and exploration of perspective, issues that are, in turn, traceable to specific elements in the finished piece, such as the checkerboard and various architectural references. One of the most exciting aspects of the piece is the way that Sfirri and Forsyth have been able to mesh their individual design aesthetics to give three-dimensional form to the ideas and imagery in the journal. Journal entries are usually by their nature, loose and exploratory, and open to multiple interpretation. Sfirri and Forsyth have very successfully carried that quality forward into the finished piece. The format of the loose parts in a playhouse denies a traditional functional role for the piece at the same time that it reinforces the narrative potential of the work and its function as a dream-house for imaginative play.

Givin' Adolf His Props (Plate 9), Adolf Volkman and Gideon Hughes' exquisite cubist wasp nest with windows, is a machine which offers beautiful mechanics as a worthy aesthetic enterprise. Although the piece honors functional mechanics, once again, true function is sacrificed for the narrative aspects of the work. The rustically built slatted cabinet incorporates multiple overlapping perspectives further complicated by windows that imply a whole other set of vanishing points. The machined crank-handle offers the viewer a place to interact with the piece. Cranking the handle opens and closes the various windows. But more than that, it leads the eye to the interior, which is filled with various drive shafts, belts, pulleys and tension devices. In this cabinet of curiosities, there is no need for exotic objects from far-away lands. Instead, *Givin' Adolf His Props* succeeds as a celebration of the wonder of mechanics and as an illustration of both makers' enthusiasm for visible, direct, and tactile mechanical systems. In the end, the piece is a celebration by two makers with different aesthetics, who clearly respect each other's working processes and share a common sense of joy and wonder in the collaborative creative process.

William Leete and Sam Chung's *Holon Form* (Plate 1) also starts with traditional furniture forms. There is a wall cabinet with four storage areas and a wall-mounted shelf which provides 9 smaller storage areas for Chung's ceramic forms. Leete and Chung made ceramic and wood "props" for interaction that explore sensuous form and changeable geometry. The turned pieces are particularly "wondrous" in that the purely abstract shapes can be combined to create convex or concave structures, while some combinations begin to suggest vessel forms that invite the viewer to place the smaller ceramic forms inside. A particularly appealing aspect of the piece is the perfectly resolved and sensuous pressure-fit of the wooden parts into the fabric-lined cabinet cavities (no matter which way they are turned and inserted). The cabinet and shelf serve as a stage upon which the viewer can move the "actors." The way the seemingly simple geometries come together to make complex and highly varied forms is particularly compelling. The piece also represents an intensive exploration of two very different materials and a search for a common language that allow the materials to work well together. The surface of the wooden objects is especially successful in that it seems to hide all its wood-like qualities. It's hard to identify, yet irresistible to touch. These collaborators suggest that an object of curiosity doesn't have to be exotic or shocking or scientifically provocative. Instead aesthetic curiosity about materials and form may be the most appropriate way to exercise wonder in the 21st century. It's a modest claim that stands in sharp contrast to the showmanship of Damien Hirst, but the quiet integrity of *Holon Form* makes their case effectively.

Kurt Nielsen and Dan Essig's *Seven Wonders* cabinet (Plate 2) makes innovative use of the traditional cabinet of curiosity vocabulary. Starting with a brilliantly constructed cabinet that is a wonder in itself, Nielsen and Essig filled each of seven alcoves with seven handmade and text-less "books." Each alcove also has a thick door, with each book and door functioning as a pair of containers for the early life stage (in the book) and the later life stage (in the door) of a different life form. The process of working one's way through the piece is intensely rewarding as it reveals all of its layered secrets slowly over the course of an extended exploration. The seven books all have a different look and feel. Each one is an aesthetic pleasure to examine and to handle. Although the magnetic push catches give away this piece's recent construction date, it has a timeless quality that works well with its presentation of the beauty and fragility of life. In its celebration of the mysteries of nature and lifecycles, and in the magical way the piece reveals its contents gradually over time, this cabinet is perhaps the most direct descendant of the traditional cabinet of curiosity in this show.

Cirque de Cabinet (Plate 5), a collaborative effort by Michael Brolly, John Biggs, Zac Robbins, Chris Coggiano, Tony Delong, and Lynne E. Brolly, stands out for its embrace of modern technology. Incorporating computer control systems and motion sensors to manage the animation of its "creature," it ventures a strong opinion about what a wondrous artifact looks like in the digital age. *Cirque de Cabinet* nominates technology as the wonder of the 21st century. The aesthetic is all-inclusive, with a variety of disparate elements combined into a form of post-modern "collage." For this group of collaborators, a modern cabinet of curiosity incorporates movement and sound. It also interacts directly with the viewer as it senses and responds to the viewer's movements. Through its idiosyncratic responses to its own observation, *Cirque de Cabinet* questions who is in charge as digital technology gets both more sophisticated and more accessible to the maker tinkering in his or her workshop. The wonder in this cabinet is also very much about what one doesn't see. The combination of miniaturization and the non-mechanical nature of the technology leaves us wondering: How does it do that? We are left to wonder at both what is and isn't there.

Two objects in this selection engage more in the celebration of the creative process than in the *Cabinets of Curiosities* concepts. They are:

The piece called *Storybook* (Plate 10), by Michelle Holzapfel, David Holzapfel, Donna C. Hawes, Dan MacArthur, Kim Thayer, Steve Smith, and Brown and Roberts Hardware, honors the creative process and the creative community that nurtured each stage of the piece's creation. It pays tribute to collaboration and community in its meticulous documentation of each stage of the creation of the piece. It uses the book as a central metaphor for knowledge. One book provides documentation of who participated and how the piece was made. A second book offers a place for viewers to add to the piece's history. Carved trompe l'oeil books hint at old-world craft and the historical knowledge we preserve in book form. More than being a cabinet of curiosities, this piece is a cabinet that expresses its makers' curiosity about how objects come to be by offering exquisite detailed documentation of one journey from concept to completion.

Top Secrets (Plate 7) by Kelly DeLor and Christopher Weiland is a fully functional storage unit for a set of custom-made spinning tops. It is a pleasure to use. A simple yet elegant door hinging system and other exposed mechanics lead the viewer logically through the process of removing or returning a top to its custom-made home. All functional aspects of the piece are fully dictated by the makers. Collaboration and the creative process itself are the driving concepts behind this piece. Christopher Weiland, the senior maker, allowed Kelly DeLor, his six-year-old collaborator, to set the initial tone of the work through her surface treatments on the tops. His cabinet both responds to and respects the wonder and spontaneous quality of her youthful creative process.

The pieces discussed above are an entirely too small selection from a terrifically diverse and innovative body of work. One of the most successful aspects of the show is the way that the combination of collaboration and subject matter (cabinets of curiosities) generated work that would not otherwise have come out of these makers' studios. As one looks at the show, one sees familiar elements of various makers' visual vocabularies, but the finished pieces often represent new directions for these makers. Another common thread in quite a number of the pieces is the suggestion that an important element of the 21st-century sense of wonder is the celebration of the creative process itself. These cabinets and the wonders they contain are not flashy or shocking like a Damien Hirst piece and they do not present scientific or biological oddities like the historical pieces. Instead they make the intriguing claim that a well-conceived and well-executed exploration of collaboration and creativity is in itself a wondrous object appropriate for the 21st century.

---

[1] Lawrence Weschler, *Mr. Wilson's Cabinet of Wonder* (New York: Vintage Books, 1995), pp. 80-81.

Provoking Wonder in the New World

—Brock Jobe

Professor of American Decorative Arts,
Winterthur Museum

Brock Jobe, who spent two decades as a museum curator and administrator, has been teaching graduate courses at Winterthur in historic interiors and American decorative arts since October 2000. His previous posts included those of research assistant at the Museum of Fine Arts, Boston, curator of exhibition buildings at Colonial Williamsburg, chief curator at the Society for the Preservation of New England Antiquities, and deputy director for collections, conservation, and interpretation at Winterthur. In his present role, he mentors students in the Winterthur Program in Early American Culture, and is also a frequent lecturer at museums, antiques shows, and collectors' clubs throughout the country. He is also the author of numerous books and essays on early American furniture and upholstery, 18th-century domestic interiors, and historic house management.

Cabinets of Curiosities. The words evoke images of delight and awe. One conjures a container filled with objects of natural or man-made wonder, or a room stuffed with a rich array of rarities. Ancient relics and animal heads, exotic shells and dazzling gems take their place with pictures and figures of every sort. Such contents become a "theatre of the broadest scope, containing authentic materials and precise reproductions of the whole of the universe," wrote a late 16th-century European scholar.[1] As the concept gained popularity, it took on many forms, but at its heart for the past five centuries, the cabinet of curiosities has remained a personal statement of its creator, a fascinating glimpse into his mind as he seeks to understand and define his world. This collaborative exhibition of the Wood Turning Center and The Furniture Society presents the work of fourteen present-day creators. In nearly every case, the builder is actually a team of individuals, who meld many techniques—most notably turning and furnituremaking— into a single work of art. Their results are as varied as their imagination and skill. Yet all of the pieces share common goals: They place objects within boundaries; these settings present individual worlds that surprise and engage; and through their diverse designs they capture a sense of the marvelous that was so characteristic of the earliest cabinets of curiosities. As they pull the viewer into the maker's universe, they can provoke, amuse, or intrigue. They demand close scrutiny and contemplation, but offer visual and intellectual rewards. Such attributes spring from a lengthy historical tradition that enables us to better appreciate the achievements of these contemporary cabinets of curiosities.

The European origins of the form can be traced back to the *studiolo* of the late 15th century. These small private chambers in the princely palaces of Northern Italy held priceless antiquities as well as the finest products of local craftsmen. For their owners, the rooms became statements of prestige, linking present-day grandeur to the accomplishments of the Ancients.[2] A shift in motivation had occurred by the middle of the 16th century, and the cabinet of curiosities, as we know it, had begun to appear. Scholars set out to assemble and preserve the material remains of their universe. The cabinet thus became the site of collection and display, where the whole of nature could be gathered in microcosm and studied in detail. Many of these initial seekers were physicians and apothecaries, driven by an interest in the medicinal properties of the world's vast array of plant and animal materials. Connoisseurs from the merchant class appropriated the concept, and royalty quickly followed suit.

The term, cabinet of curiosities, came to have two meanings. The form could be confined to a single piece of furniture adorned with shells, minerals, and cameos. German *Kunstschrank*, or "art cupboards," displayed a dazzling use of exotic woods, precious stones, and representations of the wonders of the world.[3] But the concept could also encompass an entire room (or group of rooms), typically tucked amidst the private apartments of a stately house. Such spaces came to be called, in German, *Kunstkammer*, meaning "chamber of art," or *Wunderkammer*, "chamber of marvels," and served as retreats for study and contemplation—places to be shared only with the knowledgeable and by special invitation. The array of curiosities reached dizzying proportions; rooms were crammed with a mélange of media. Yet the organization was not haphazard. Their creators sought order in their presentation and arranged their collections with geometric precision. Such symmetry and balance reinforced their own belief in an orderly world. Collectors further defined the plan of the space through careful classification. They labeled cases and identified specific items. And as their holdings grew, they gathered materials with the watchful eye of the scientist ever on the lookout for the new and the different—items that could enhance their understanding of the world.

The contents of these cabinets fell into two broad categories: *Naturalia*, the products of nature, and

Figure 8
The Indian Hall, Monticello,
Charlottesville, Virginia

Artificialia, the wonders of man. Yet hybrid forms combining art and nature became a key part of the collector's world. Conch shells cradled in a gold frame or ostrich eggs mounted on a silver-gilt stand found their way into royal cabinets. And even in more modest cabinets, owners sometimes enhanced an unadorned fragment of nature. The approach, regardless of the individual, tended toward the miraculous, the rare, and the exotic. The Archduke Ferdinand II of Tyrol (1520–1595) assembled the quintessential cabinet, filling three rooms with more than a thousand objects ranging from scientific instruments and ancient medals to stuffed sharks, lizards, and the representation of a dwarf and giant. The presence of the very small and the very large was a familiar theme, repeated frequently in many cabinets (another ranged from insects to dinosaur bones). In every respect, Ferdinand's eclectic taste for natural wonders, grand art, bizarre monsters, and human freaks reflected the wide-ranging passion of the most active collectors.[4]

The New World offered a vast source of material for European cabinets. Flowers and seeds, birds and animals (either living or preserved), and fossil and mineral specimens all aroused enormous interest. But probably nothing generated more excitement than the tools, clothing, and products of Native Americans. So different from the garments and goods of Europeans, these objects startled and intrigued the collector. Their strange appearance and ingenious workmanship provoked many comments; frequently too, they were accompanied by spectacular stories of acquisition. One notable cabinet of the third-quarter of the 17th century, curated by the German Jesuit Athanasius Kircher (1602–1680) in Rome, included among its most treasured possessions Brazilian necklaces, birch-bark ladles, and "masks of the inhabitants of Canada"; another had Amazonian war axes and "flutes made of legs which have been eaten by the cannibals."[5] Adventurers made their way to the Americas, not only to study but also to send back samples of the flora and fauna of this immense region. In the 18th century, naturalists such as Mark Catesby and Peter Kalm made extended visits, and native sons John and William Bartram traveled widely in search of rare species. Perhaps the most industrious of these scholar-collectors was the royal physician Hans Sloane (1660–1753), who acquired 12,500 botanical specimens during his visits to the West Indies. His far-flung interests and unquenchable passion for things led him to accumulate over 100,000 items, a vast holding which eventually became the foundation of the British Museum.[6]

In colonial America, modest cabinets could be found in the homes of prominent and intellectually curious gentlemen and clerics. Better documentation for such repositories, however, appears in the accounts of the newly formed colleges. Harvard College traces the origins of a cabinet to 1672, when it received a telescope from Governor John Winthrop.[7] Subsequent donors deposited an odd assortment of Naturalia. During a visit to the college in 1744, Alexander Hamilton noted that the library included a sizable collection of books as well as "some curiositys, the best of which is the cut of a tree about 10 inches thick and eight long, entirely petrified and turned into stone."[8] In Philadelphia, the prolific Benjamin Franklin founded two institutions that formed cabinets of their own. During the 1750s, the Library Company received a collection of Eskimo garments from a local ship captain who had traveled to the Artic. By 1768, the American Philosophical Society had charged a committee "to get made a Cabinet suitable for keeping the Curiosities &c. belonging to the Society."[9] Contributors throughout the Colonies submitted materials. Natural history specimens predominated; other gifts ranged from fossils to models of new inventions. Like their European counterparts, colonists also pursued Native American material. But they also sought objects of historical significance, particularly those relating to their own political past. By the early 19th century, the Society's cabinet included the writing arm Windsor chair upon which Thomas

Jefferson wrote the Declaration of Independence.[10]

The cabinets of the American Philosophical Society and Library, as well as those formed by other institutions at the time, remained the special preserve of their members. But a movement was underfoot to give similar collections a more public face. In 1782, the Swiss painter Pierre Eugene du Simitiere (1737–1784) announced the opening of his "American Museum" in Philadelphia. For the price of one-half dollar, anyone could see his collection. Tours were offered five times a day, four days a week. Like the collectors of Europe, du Simitiere divided his holdings into natural and artificial curiosities. Among the former, he offered marine "productions," such as shells, sea-eggs, coral, and crabs, and land "productions," ranging from worms to rare birds. He also displayed an array of fossils and petrified specimens as well as a collection of exotic West Indian plants. His artificial curiosities included European weapons, Indian clothing, and "Musical Instruments and Utensils of the Negroes, from the coast of Guinea, and the West Indies." He ended his list with his own work: a collection of paintings in oil, crayon, watercolor, miniature, and "a curious deception of perspective." Du Simitiere's museum perfectly parallels the historic traditions of the cabinet of curiosities. Its contents were intended to surprise and delight, to provoke wonder at the world's variety and eccentricities. Though named the American Museum, the collections bore much in common with Old World models. Du Simitiere undoubtedly hoped to ride on the coattails of revolutionary patriotism, and indeed his museum did enjoy modest success. But his premature death in 1784 brought an end to the institution, the first public museum in the United States.[11]

The concept of a public museum remained a viable one in Philadelphia. Less than two years after du Simitiere's passing, the painter Charles Willson Peale (1741–1827) opened his own museum. Like his predecessor, Peale pursued the project for financial reasons. He could not support himself and his family solely through his painting business and turned to the museum for additional income. In Peale's case, the results were far more successful. For the next forty years, Peale and his children operated America's best-known public museum. Its goals mirrored those of its founder. It was a place of erudition and learning where a structured and orderly universe could be viewed in miniature through the thousands of objects that eventually entered the collection. Both founder and institution promoted social harmony within a prescribed hierarchy. Through his writings and indirectly through his exhibitions, Peale urged wives to defer to their husbands, blacks to accept subordination to whites. Though public in the sense that admission only required a ticket, the museum was not democratic. The audience consisted of mostly well-to-do, white males from the ranks of merchants, professionals, and craftsmen. For these viewers, Peale presented a mix of curiosities reminiscent of traditional cabinets. In many cases, he heightened the effect of his stranger or abnormal items by placing them behind a curtain. A deformed cow—*The Cow with 5 legs, 6 feet and two tails*—remained veiled, waiting for those who wanted to experience the shock of its appearance, but easily bypassed by others.[12] Like keepers of earlier cabinets, Peale carefully controlled his environment.

Donations to Peale's Museum came from near and far. One prominent figure, Thomas Jefferson, not only provided numerous objects but also served as president of the museum's Board of Visitors. Jefferson's own collecting efforts offer a fascinating comparison with that of Peale. Though more focused than the omnivorous Peale, Jefferson had a seemingly insatiable interest in the natural wonders of his native Virginia, the artifacts of Native Americans, and the cultivation of classical antiquity. The master of Monticello epitomized the learned gentleman of his day. In the words of Francis Bacon, written nearly two centuries earlier, certain attributes characterized such men:

"First, the collecting of a most perfect and general library, wherein whosoever the wit of man hath heretofore committed to books of worth . . . may be made contributory to your wisdom. Next, a spacious, wonderful garden . . . so you may have in small compass a model of the universal nature made private. The third, a goodly, huge cabinet, wherein whatsoever the hand of man by exquisite art or engine has made rare in stuff, form or motion; whatsoever singularity, chance, and the shuffle of things hath produced; whatsoever Nature has wrought in things that want life and may be kept; shall be sorted and included."[13]

Jefferson's love of learning and gardening have long been recognized, but his efforts to create a cabinet of rarities wrought by man or nature has only recently attracted attention.[14] The entrance hall at Monticello—the most public of all spaces in the house—became Jefferson's cabinet of curiosities. He often referred to the room as his Indian Hall and hung it with European paintings and sculpture, Indian maps and artifacts acquired by Lewis and Clark, the head and horns of elk, deer, buffalo, and even the fossilized bones of a mammoth or mastodon. In Jefferson's mind, the scale of the mammoth demonstrated the grandeur of America. For further emphasis, he mounted the jawbones and tusk of an elephant nearby; the giant of the New World dwarfed his counterpart of the Old.

Jefferson arranged the hundreds of artifacts in the room with meticulous precision. According to an account of 1815, one wall was covered "with curiosities which Lewis and Clark found in their wild and perilous expedition."[15] Another was apparently devoted to natural history, and the other two to a fine arts gallery of painting and sculpture. Like cabinets of the past (and indeed like that of his friend Peale), the Indian Hall presented the collector's world in miniature. Through the selection and placement of objects, it also conveyed Jefferson's admiration for America and respect for classical antiquity. But in contrast to the private spaces of Francis Bacon and other early collectors, Jefferson's cabinet of curiosities was open to all who visited. To be sure, one often had to travel a considerable distance and needed the proper credentials to call at Monticello, but for those who made the journey, they had a startling surprise in store as they entered the house. The experience often left a memorable impression. As a visitor noted, there was "no private gentleman in the world in possession of so perfect and complete a scientific, useful and ornamental collection."[16]

After Jefferson's death, a few pieces from his ethnographic and natural history collections were given to Peale's Museum while the rest were transferred to the University of Virginia. Though most have since disappeared, several important items have been returned over the past fifty years. These include elk and moose antlers along with a few of the mastodon bones. Recently Elizabeth Chew, associate curator at Monticello, coordinated the reinstallation of the Indian Hall, using a combination of original and reproduction objects. Now, for the first time since the 1820s, the dramatic intent of Jefferson's plan for this grand public space can be understood and appreciated.

Within Europe, the cabinet of curiosities achieved its greatest popularity over a two-century period stretching from about 1550 until 1750. The phenomenon continued in America, particularly in institutions and intellectual circles, into the early years of the 19th century. But increased understanding of the natural world, the development of more specialized collections, and the appropriation of more detailed classification systems led to the separation of many personal and university collections into discrete entities that focused either on natural history, cultural history, or fine arts and eventually to the creation of the modern museum.

Yet the concept of individual cabinets filled with a pastiche of personal possessions remains a powerful one. Arguably, it inspired 20th-century artists such as Andre Breton and Joseph Cornell to develop their own unique interpretations.[17] In more recent years, it has sparked numerous exhibitions, some celebrating past achievements, others spurring new versions of the traditional form. The Hood Museum at Dartmouth College explored the spectacular qualities of Late Renaissance and Baroque European cabinets and their contents in a groundbreaking exhibition, *The Age of the Marvelous*, which traveled to Atlanta, Houston, and Raleigh from the fall of 1991 through the winter of 1993.[18] Five years later, the National Gallery of Art mounted *A Collector's Cabinet*, an intimate recreation of a 17th-century Dutch cabinet. Though only occupying three small galleries, this gem-like display attracted more than 230,000 visitors over a five-month period.[19] Other shows have used the traditional goals of a cabinet as the impetus to the creation of new works. Like their predecessors, these recent productions are personal and often eccentric; they present a container for defining their world, for providing a sense of order, and for celebrating the fantastic, the wondrous, and the marvelous. *Cabinets of Curiosities, Four Artists, Four Visions*, which opened on October 7, 2000, at the Elvehjem Museum of Art, presented the work of Martha Glowacki, Mark Lorenzi, Natasha Nicholson, and Mary Alice Wimmer.[20] Their extraordinary assemblages differ dramatically but reveal their makers' common interest in observation, collecting, and organization—all key attributes of classic cabinets of curiosities.

In 2003, the Wood Turning Center and Furniture Society adopted a similar theme, but with qualifications. First, each artist was encouraged to collaborate. That combination of talents took various forms. Miguel Gomez-Ibañez sought the assistance of a painter, Joseph Reed. Amy Forsyth, an architect and furnituremaker, joined forces with the turner Mark Sfirri. Gideon Hughes fashioned a frame for pattern-maker Adolf Volkman. Only Gordon Peteran worked alone, but driven, as he said, by two inner voices, one of the cabinetmaker, the other of the turner.

Second, each team was asked to include both turning and furnituremaking in its work. Again the solutions differed from project to project. In *Round Guy Meets Square Guy* (Plate 12), Michael Hosaluk and Mitch Ryerson contrast the turned ball with the square box—the ultimate craft dialectic. Gordon Peteran also juxtaposes primary shapes as his chest emerges from a bowl. Christopher Weiland fills a narrow cabinet with turned spinning tops that are decorated by six-year-old Kelly DeLor—all the while "exploring cabinet forms that are playful and simple . . . [and seeking] to capture a complementing balance of imagery between Kelly's work and mine."[21] A less obvious combination of techniques appears in *Holon Form* (Plate 1) by William Leete and Sam Chung. The cabinet structure is balanced by vessel forms that are made of two faceplate turnings, which have been cut in half, carved, and reassembled in a new arrangement.

Though unmistakably dissimilar in their appearance, the fourteen cabinets chosen for the exhibition share many traits with their traditional counterparts. Most importantly, they have a container and contents. The container is a single form, rather than a room, and in this sense they recall the *Kunstschrank* of 17th-century Germany. The cabinets accommodate a remarkable spectrum of objects, which collectively offer fascinating pictures of their makers' world. The containers for Doug Haslam's *Ein Kleiner Wunderschrank* (Plate 6) and Kurt Nielsen and Dan Essig's *Seven Wonders* (Plate 2) illustrate the range—from a rectangular cabinet to a stand and cylinder surmounted by a turned and carved globe. One relates indirectly to medieval reliquaries, the other to *To Pao Ko*, Chinese boxes of plain form with complex interiors. In both cases, objects are hidden from sight, waiting to be discovered by the viewer. A more obvious relationship between container and contents appears in Po Shun Leong *Time Standing Still* (Plate 8). Found objects culled from the studio of the late Bob Stocksdale provide flesh to the bones of the case. A turned ebony bowl forms the heart.

Next, these contemporary cabinets retain the sense of surprise that epitomizes the historical form. Certainly Michael Brolly's *Cirque de Cabinet* (Plate 5) startles in its shapes, colors, and irreverent manner. Gideon Hughes and Adolf Volkman disguise the intricacy of their form, clothing complicated mechanical pullies and gears with a cartoon-like shell (*Givin' Adolf His Props,* Plate 9).

And Michelle Holzapfel creates an air of mystery and marvel through her trompe l'oeil *Story Book* (Plate 10). Such deceptions often were a key component of early cabinets, particularly Dutch versions of the 17th century.

Third, all of the current examples reflect the individual personalities of their makers. Though historic versions frequently had similar components, the final compendium of materials remained a singular expression. Individual collectors went to extraordinary lengths to obtain unusual objects and infuse their own stamp on their cabinets. Today, this unique vision may come from a story contained in the contents, as Michelle Holzapfel provides through woods and pictures in *Story Book*, or as Amy Forsyth and Mark Sfirri introduce in *"Figurati . . . "* (*"go figure yourself"*) (Plate 4). Other artists turn to common themes of historic cabinets, but explore them in distinctive, sometimes playful, ways. Exotic dried flowers and seeds were a popular curiosity of many baroque cabinets. In *Seeds of Curiosity: Staples of Transformation* (Plate 14), Jack Larimore and Stephen Hogbin offer their own distinctive view of the importance of seeds as a staple for the world's survival, placing tiny vials of seeds within an exaggerated seedpod of immense scale.

Finally, these present-day cabinets adhere, in varying degrees, to their forebears' commitment to order. Historically, knowledge was valued, and contemplation was encouraged. Collections of curiosities provided unparalleled opportunities for empirical learning. One could study the world in all its variety, but come to recognize its overall structure. Certainly the beauty of order is captured in three works: Chris Becksvoort and Alex Dulberg's *Threads Of Simplicity* (Plate 3), a striking expression of the Shaker plain style, Miguel Gomez-Ibañez's *Vargueño* (Plate 13), a playful version of a classic Spanish form, and William Leete and Sam Chung's *Holon Form* (Plate 1), a stylized flower filled with graceful shapes.

As a student of 18th-century American furniture, I have long been interested in traditional crafts. I marvel at the efficiency and sure-handedness of the best colonial artisans. Yet the quality of their work cannot begin to approach that of the makers of European cabinets of curiosities. The metalsmiths, jewelers, painters, carvers, and joiners who fashioned the best *Kunstschrank* were men of immense talent. Their skillful manipulation of materials, coupled with the wonders of nature and the ancient world contained in such cabinets, resulted in breathtaking objects. Today's studio furniture and turned wood movements strive in their own way for much the same effect. Exceptionally proficient artists create imaginative designs that provoke wonder and excitement. These individuals strive to achieve their own personals statements. In *Cabinets of Curiosities*, we have given fourteen teams of such artists the opportunity to create microcosms of their world. In the process, they have illuminated our own.

[1] Quoted in Patrick Mauries, *Cabinets of Curiosities* (London: Thames & Hudson, 2002), p. 23.

[2] Ibid., pp. 52-55, 65.

[3] Ibid., pp. 56-63.

[4] Ibid., pp. 132-34; Elisabeth Scheicher, "The Collection of Archduke Ferdinand II at Schloss Ambras: Its Purpose, Composition and Evolution," in Oliver Impey and Arthur MacGregor, eds., *The Origins of Museums, The Cabinet of Curiosities in Sixteenth- and Seventeenth-Century Europe* (Oxford: Clarendon Press, 1985), pp. 29-38.

[5] Quoted in Joy Kenseth, "A World of Wonders in One Closet Shut," in Joy Kenseth, ed., *The Age of the Marvelous* (Hanover, New Hampshire: Hood Museum of Art, 1991), p. 91; for information on Kircher, see also William Schupbach, "Some Cabinets of Curiosities in European Academic Institutions," in Impey and MacGregor, eds., *The Origins of Museums*, pp. 174-75; Mauries, *Cabinets of Curiosities*, 160-63.

[6] Arthur MacGregor, "The Cabinet of Curiosities in Seventeenth-Century Britain," in Impey and MacGregor, eds., *The Origins of Museums*, p. 157; see also J. C. H. King, "North American Ethnography in the Collection of Sir Hans Sloane," in the same volume, pp. 232-36.

[7] Joel J. Orosz, *Curators and Culture: The Museum Movement in America, 1740–1870* (Tuscaloosa and London: The University of Alabama Press, 1990), p. 17.

[8] Carl Bridenbaugh, ed., *Gentleman's Progress, The Itinerarium of Dr. Alexander Hamilton, 1744* (Chapel Hill: University of North Carolina Press, 1948), p. 142.

[9] Orosz, *Curators and Culture*, p. 16. The order for the cabinet is quoted in Whitfield J. Bell, Jr., "The Cabinet of the American Philosophical Society," in *A Cabinet of Curiosities, Five Episodes in the Evolution of American Museums* (Charlottesville: The University Press of Virginia, 1967), p. 3. The actual order was initiated by the American Society, but probably implemented by the American Philosophical Society, after the two organizations merged during the winter of 1768–69.

[10] Bell, "The Cabinet of the American Philosophical Society," p. 16.

[11] Orosz, *Curators and Culture*, p. 30-43.

[12] Quoted in David R. Brigham, *Public Culture in the Early Republic, Peale's Museum and Its Audience* (Washington and London: Smithsonian Institution Press, 1995), p. 147; see also pp. 145-50.

[13] Quoted in Joyce Henri Robinson, "An American Cabinet of Curiosities, Thomas Jefferson's Indian Hall at Monticello," *Winterthur Portfolio* 30, no. 1 (Spring 1995): 43.

[14] Ibid., pp. 41-58.

[15] Quoted in ibid., p. 47.

[16] Quoted in ibid., p. 49.

[17] Mauries, *Cabinets of Curiosities*, pp. 214-19, 225-27.

[18] See Kenseth, *The Age of the Marvelous*.

[19] See Arthur K. Wheelock, Jr., *A Collector's Cabinet* (Washington, D. C.: National Gallery of Art, 1998).

[20] See *Cabinets of Curiosities, Four Visions, Four Artists* (Madison: Elvehjem Museum of Art, University of Wisconsin, 2000). Catalogue essays were contributed by Joseph Goldyne and Thomas H. Garver; the exhibition was organized by Natasha Nicholson.

[21] Correspondence, Christopher Weiland to Teresa Curran of the Wood Turning Center, July 21, 2002.

The Plates

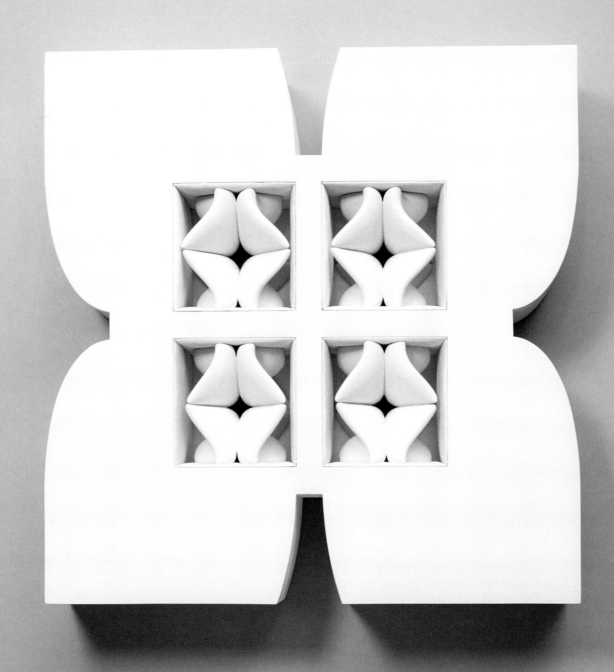

PLATE 1

[detail]

Holon Form, 2002
William Leete and Sam Chung, USA

PLATE 2

[detail]

Seven Wonders, 2002
Kurt Nielsen and Dan Essig, USA

PLATE 3

[detail]

Threads Of Simplicity, 2002
Chris Becksvoort and Alex Dulberg, USA

PLATE 4

[detail]

"Figurati . . . " ("go figure yourself"), 2002
Amy Forsyth and Mark Sfirri, USA

PLATE 5

[detail]

Cirque de Cabinet, 2003
Michael Brolly, John Biggs, Zac Robbins,
Chris Coggiano, Tony Delong, and Lynne E. Brolly, all USA

PLATE 6

[detail]

Ein Kleiner Wunderschrank (*micro thaumata*), 2002
Doug Haslam, Linda Chow, Fred Coates, Jeff DeBoer, Debra Yelva
Dedyluk, Mark Dicey, Gordon Galenza, Trudy Golley, Christina Greco,
Crys Harse, Bonny Houston, Paul Leathers, Kari McQueen,
Les Pinter, Colleen Rauscher, Bruce Watson, and Louise Williamson,
all Canada

PLATE 7

[detail]

Top Secrets, 2002
Christopher Weiland and Kelly DeLor, USA

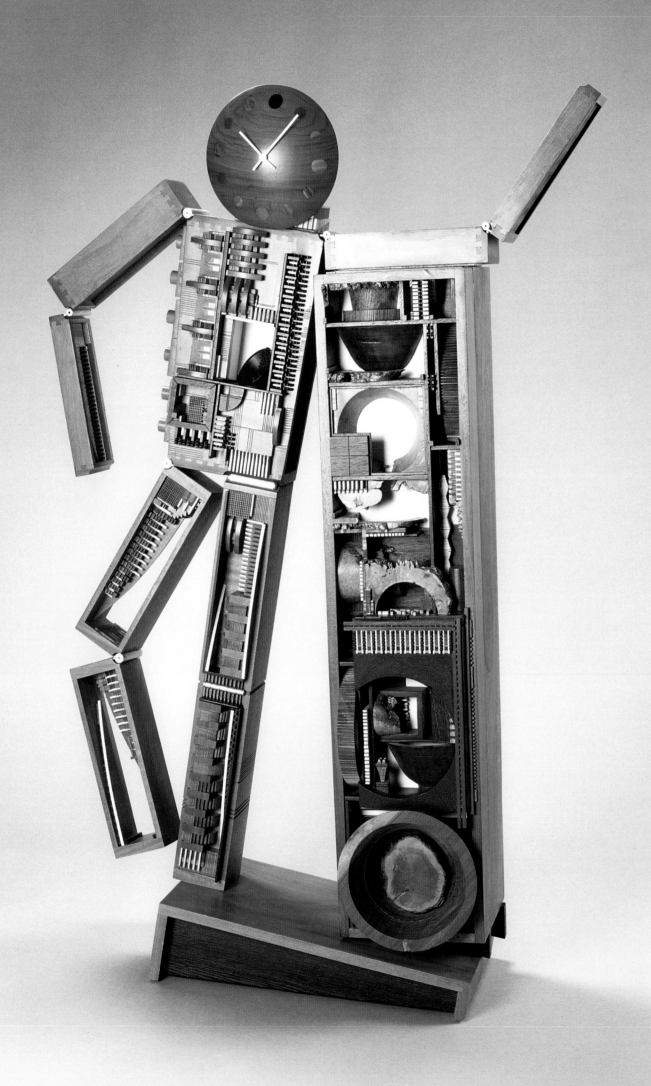

PLATE 8

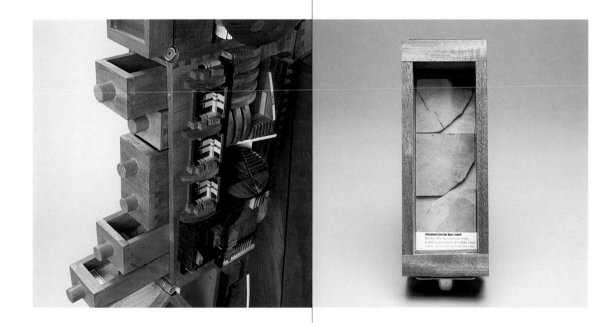

[detail]

Time Standing Still, 2002
Po Shun Leong and Bob Stocksdale, USA

PLATE 9

[detail]

Givin' Adolf His Props, 2002
Gideon Hughes and Adolf Volkman, USA

PLATE 10

[detail]

Story Book, 2002
Michelle Holzapfel, David Holzapfel,
Donna C. Hawes, Dan MacArthur, Kim Thayer,
Steve Smith, and Brown & Roberts Hardware, all USA

PLATE 11

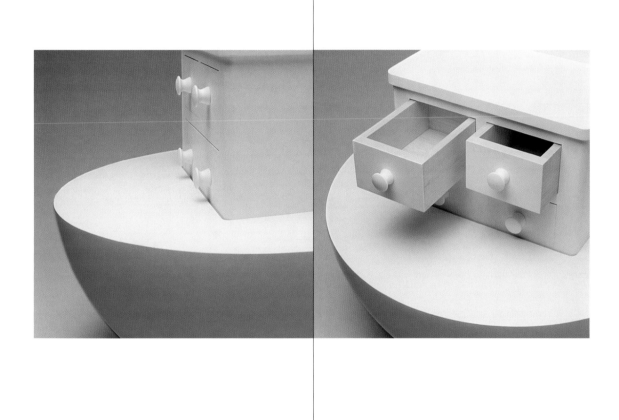

[detail]

Chest in a Bowl, 2002
Gordon Peteran, Canada

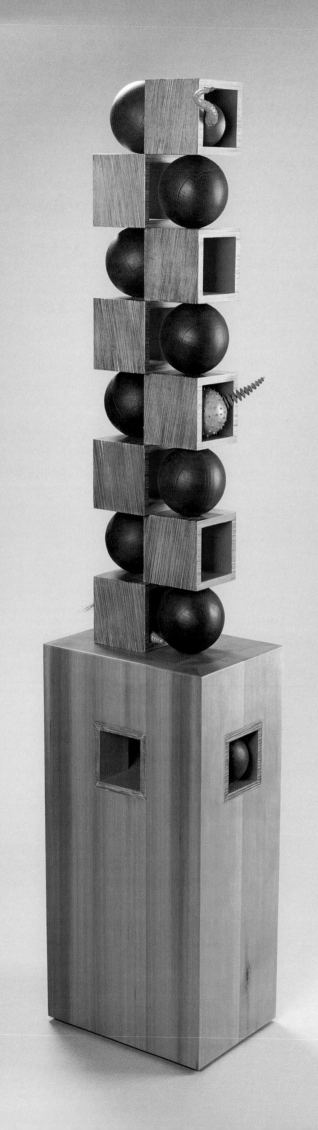

PLATE 12

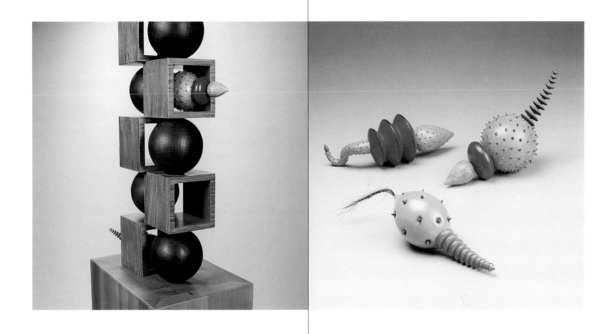

[detail]

Round Guy Meets Square Guy, 2000
Michael Hosaluk, Canada; Mitch Ryerson, USA

PLATE 13

[detail]

Vargueño, 2002
Miguel Gomez-Ibañez and Joseph Reed, USA

PLATE 14

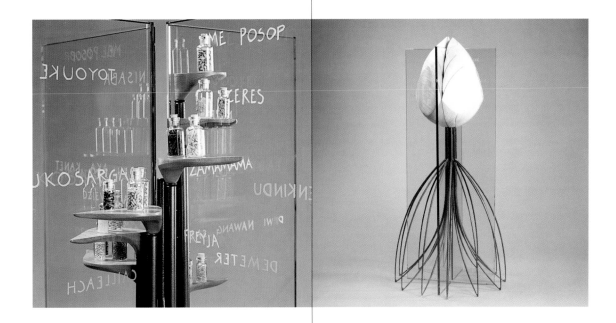

[detail]

Seeds of Curiosity: Staples of Transformation, 2002
Jack Larimore, USA; Stephen Hogbin, Canada

Genesis

Plate 1

William Leete and Sam Chung, USA
Holon Form
2002
Wood, ceramic, epoxy, paint, and fabric
46 x 31 x 8 in.

Our main thought behind this work is the concept of holons. Holons are whole/parts. Everything being a holon means that everything is made up of parts and simultaneously part of a greater whole. (Primary source of concept is the writing of philosopher Ken Wilber.) In our work it's obvious that there is a hierarchy of parts creating systems within systems. We are interested in providing a variety of relationships among numerous parts that express a sense of growth and multiplication. We deliberately chose shapes that suggest budding and bulging plant and animal forms. Ultimately this work is an interactive sculpture about relationships between wholes and parts. The participation of the user creates a larger whole than the static work by itself.

—William Leete, Sam Chung

Plate 2
Kurt Nielsen and Dan Essig, USA
Seven Wonders
2002
Cabinet: mahogany, rubber wood, pommelle sapele, 23-karat gold, clay, silk, mica, brass nails, carved, burnt, hammered, acrylic, milk paint, oil stains, aniline dyes, lacquer, varnish, luna moth, cicada shell, leaf skeleton, mulberry, horse shoe crab, sea shells, and Roman bronze arrowheads
Books: mahogany, mica, brass nails, hand-made cotton paper, linen thread, flax, velvet, leather, brass, milk paint, wax, luna moth pupa, seventeen-year cicada, fossilized ferns, mulberry, Kozo paper, bone, trilobite, ammonites, and stone arrowheads
64 x 23 x 23 in.

The books I make are blank and I have never kept a journal. Nevertheless, my books house thousands of objects that I have collected since childhood. Rocks, fossils, coins, shells, and seed pods are all part of an unwritten diary that I keep. These small and insignificant souvenirs tell the story of a life spent walking through woods and caves, a search along the side of a road for something to pick up and keep as a reminder of a moment, person, or place.

—Dan Essig

The majority of my work explores my personal symbols, imagery and temperaments. Most furniture by default is a container, but I begin designing by asking what is to be contained: a television or stereo, a piece of art, incriminating tax evasion documents of an employer from whom you are embezzling millions, a secret or a thought. Many of my pieces have hidden compartments within, and many have guardians to protect those objects hidden inside, whether tangible or intangible. It was the stories being told by our work, without text, and the secrets contained within that spawned this collaboration.

—Kurt Nielsen

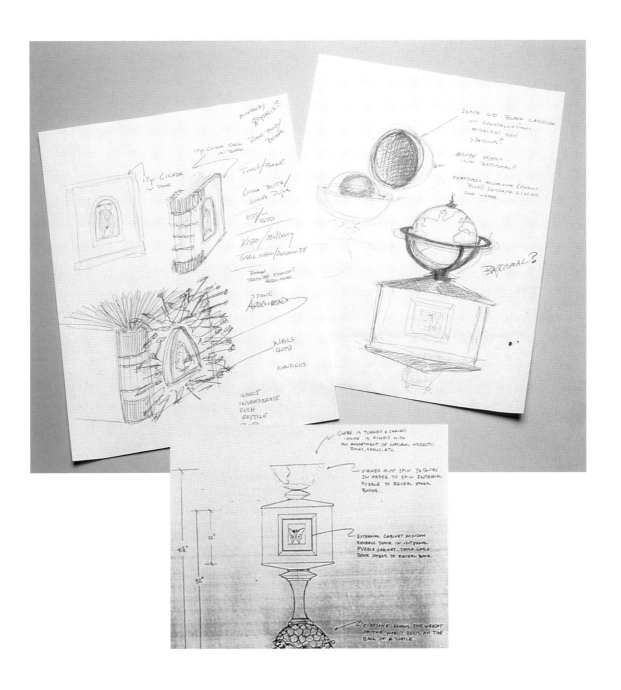

Plate 3

Chris Becksvoort and Alex Dulberg, USA
Threads Of Simplicity
2002
Maple, bird's eye maple, cherry, dogwood, hop hornbeam, apple,
walnut, plum, birch, dye, thread, steel, and brass
30 x 13 x 11 in.

My work was inspired from the onset by the workmanship of the Shakers. It humbles me to think that something as ordinary as a wooden spool would be so well made, and warrant so much effort.

From the Shaker's point of view, the spools were tools used to hold thread, nothing more, nothing less. From our point of view, a century and a half later, these spools are wooden jewels and examples of meticulous craftsmanship.

—Chris Becksvoort

Plate 4

Amy Forsyth and Mark Sfirri, USA
"Figurati . . . " (*"go figure yourself"*)
2002
Walnut, milk paint, pau amarillo, macassar ebony, purpleheart,
tulip wood, king wood, chatke kok, mahogany, maple, plywood, paper,
leather, chipboard, ink, and colored pencil
54 x 24 x 17 in.

Amy,

Are you out there? I can't even remember which direction you were headed in. How was the first
of many workshops for you? I should be out in my shop working now, but I just can't take 100
degrees. I'm too old for it. I've been thinking about our Cab. of Curiosities project. I think that it
might make life a little easier (for you especially) if I make the base of the piece (legs, rails and
drawer and the pieces to fit in them). What do you think? November seems like a long ways away,
but summer, school starting, Furniture Society programming, my grant stuff for school . . . and
on and on, it seems like this might make a clearer cut to the chase, realistic approach to the project.
All I would need to know is what are the overall dimensions of it—Height width and depth. You
could do from the tabletop and up. This way, if, heaven forbid, it doesn't sell, we'd each have a
part to take away at the end. Let me know what you think.

—Mark

Hey, Mark.

Things are moving along on the C of Cs, but slowly. I keep having to build jigs and order bits,
things like that. I'm working on the joinery for the roof trusses, and have gradually been surfacing
the wood for the "architectural elements." The frames are together—I painted the joints between
the plywood and the walnut frame before gluing them together, and that felt like progress.

—Later, Amy

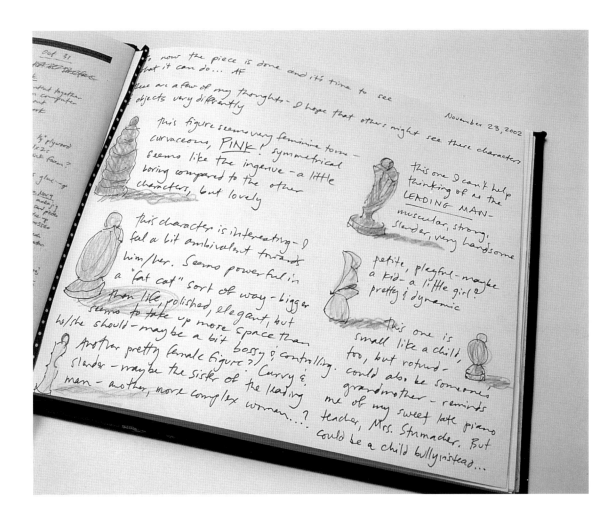

... now the piece is done and its time to see
that it can do ... AF

there are a few of my thoughts - I hope that others might see these characters
objects very differently

November 23, 2002

this figure seems very feminine to me -
curvaceous, <u>PINK</u>. symmetrical
seems like the ingenue - a little
boring compared to the other
characters, but lovely

this one I can't help
thinking of as the
<u>LEADING MAN</u> -
muscular, strong,
slender, very handsome

this character is interesting - I
feel a bit ambivalent toward
him/her. Seems powerful in
a "fat cat" sort of way - bigger
than life, polished, elegant, but
seems to take up more space than
he/she should - maybe a bit
bossy & controlling.

petite, playful - maybe
a kid - a little girl?
pretty & dynamic

Another pretty female figure? Curvy &
slender - maybe the sister of the leading
man - another, more complex woman ....?

this one is
small like a child,
too, but rotund -
could also be someone's
grandmother - reminds
me of my sweet late piano
teacher, Mrs. Strumacher. But
could be a child bully instead ...

Plate 5

Michael Brolly, John Biggs, Zac Robbins,
Chris Coggiano, Tony Delong, and Lynne E. Brolly, all USA
Cirque de Cabinet
2003
Poplar, mahogany, cherry, ply wood, nails, electric motors, electric eye,
computer chip, Lazy Susan, beads, buttons, wire, springs, glass, and
acrylic paint
32 x 20 x 20 in.

I saw John Biggs' stuff at Wexlar gallery and Lou Wexlar showed me the eyes that are in our piece. John said I could use his eyes in a collaboration, and he also agreed to do something in a bottle for the piece. Zac Robbins agreed to blow a glass belly that John could put one of his things in. Chris Coggiano had done a small drawing in the place where I buy flowers for my wife and I thought it would be cool to have him paint our piece. Lynne, being a collector of strange things herself, made more pieces for the creature's collection. Tony Delong's computerization enabled us to make more elaborate mechanizations.

Our cabinet would in itself be a curiosity while exploring the notion that what one sees as a collectible another might see in an altogether different light. Somewhere along the line of the "One man's trash is another man's cash" theme of trash haulers everywhere. Not to mention dumpster divers.

So our cabinet would be a creature, in and of itself, with animatronic eyes that are responsive to the viewer via hidden sensors. One eye would keep watch on the viewer while the other would guide the viewer to look into the creature's navel. The whole stomach section will be a hand-blown glass vessel in which is contained several different creatures that will be mounted in some fashion and most likely revolving. This will cause the viewer to wonder whether the cabinet ate them or is just storing them for material as he/she ponders his/her own navel.

—Michael Brolly

Plate 6

Doug Haslam, Linda Chow, Fred Coates, Jeff DeBoer, Debra Yelva Dedyluk, Mark Dicey, Gordon Galenza, Trudy Golley, Christina Greco, Crys Harse, Bonny Houston, Paul Leathers, Kari McQueen, Les Pinter, Colleen Rauscher, Bruce Watson, and Louise Williamson, all Canada
Ein Kleiner Wunderschrank (micro thaumata)
2002
Case: Walnut, baltic birch plywood, brass hinges and catch, and lacquer finish; Objects: Sterling silver, 18K yellow gold plate, moon stones, earth magnets, wire, feathers, fish hooks, paper, ink, slide mounts and carrier, transparencies, found objects, paint, wood, laminate, ceramic with glaze application, Rhodoid, tarantula molt, glass, copper wool, depletion silvered Sterling silver, ormolu (24Kt. gold on bronze), computer chip, lace, gauze, finger cots, iodine copper, wire, sphere magnet, lima bean, cloth, Datura pod, papier maché, pistachio shells, snail shells, flower, fabric, cat's whiskers; Inner works and object alterations: baltic birch ply, acrylic paint, cork, wire, toilet paper, sandpaper, glass beads, Maccassar ebony, Mylar, paper, Granitex, magnets, Pernambuco, aluminum and glass watchcase covers, rosewood, glass bottles, assorted spices, cigarette package foil, cheesecloth, brass hinges and screws, sea sponge, mahogany, doll eye, brass and aluminum (tube, wire and rod), hemlock, foam, rocks, photocopies (images, words and symbols), sheet steel, cherry, plastic aileron hinges, glue, gold leaf, cloth, purpleheart, iodine, wax, copper (sheet and powder), avodire, ink, thread, mirror
16 x 13 1/2 x 16 1/2 in.

I had the good fortune of coming across these miniature curio cabinets (To Pao Ko) in 1990 when I was visiting the National Palace Museum in Taipei, Taiwan. . . . I was spellbound by their variety of shapes, forms, and methods of opening as well as how the treasured objects were hidden inside of them.

These To Pao Ko were the possessions of the Ching dynasty emperors and probably derived their form from the traveling cases of Ming dynasty scholars and literati. . . . They were taken from the personal residences of the Emperor and his family and contain a variety of tiny objects intended for the enjoyment of their owner. Objects such as carvings in ivory and jade, small scrolls of painting and calligraphy, and miniature representations of brush racks and water droppers were contained in these boxes, often in secret compartments with trick latches. The boxes themselves were also intended to be used for the display of the objects. One can imagine that the process of opening these cabinets and discovering the variety of secrets that lay within was just as important as the objects themselves.

—Doug Haslam

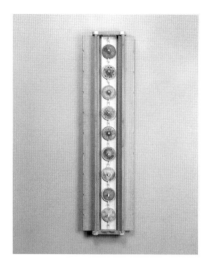

Plate 7

Christopher Weiland and Kelly DeLor, USA
Top Secrets
2002
Medium density flakeboard, maple, brass, acrylic paint, wax crayon, and colored pencil
50 x 8 1/2 x 4 in.

Now that I've had a little time to reflect upon the creation of our cabinet of curiosity, I can honestly say that this piece has been one of the most enjoyable furniture pieces I have ever constructed. Throughout each developing stage of this project, I reflected back many times to my early childhood days of playing with wooden blocks, tinker toys, model airplanes and boats, and especially discarded cardboard boxes. Working or shall I say "playing" with Kelly as my collaborating partner on this project inspired me as an artist in more ways than I ever imagined. For Kelly, color was her best friend. She used it boldly and with absolute confidence. In the past, I've always been too cautious about using color in my work. On this project, I tried Kelly's approach to using color and was far less hesitant. . . . The best results turned out to be the same color mediums as Kelly used in her disc compositions: water-based color washes, colored pencils, and crayons.

—Christopher Weiland

Plate 8
Po Shun Leong and Bob Stocksdale, USA
Time Standing Still
2002
Various wood and metal
79 x 42 x 13 in.

When the sirens screamed in London during the Second World War, we headed underground for the deep shelters to avoid the German bombs. To escape the dangers in 1944, my father sent me, as a three-year-old child, to live with a carpenter in the countryside until the end of the war.

The carpenter had a hobby of making model ocean liners. One of them, a majestically long vessel, filled his small parlor. When he carved the complex wood pieces, I crouched beside the liner and rolled marbles along the enclosed decks and into the maze of its inner chambers. . . .

In 1964, I immigrated to Mexico after receiving an architecture degree cum laude in London from the Architectural Association. For the next 16 years I designed department stores, schools and homes and produced low-cost furniture. My architectural models were important for clients to decide whether to make the projects possible.

Fifty-eight years later in California, that model wartime liner is still there to haunt my art.

—Po Shun Leong

Plate 9

Gideon Hughes and Adolf Volkman, USA
Givin' Adolf His Props
2002
Scrap wood, glass, wooden pulleys, and cranks
49 x 27 x 17 1/2 in.

Most of us take mechanics for granted. Why does a car go? Why do planes land safely? Few people know that it was often pattern makers working with wood that made it possible. Our piece is designed to feature its mechanics while also veiling its importance in shadow. I want people to see Adolf's woodworking even if you have to search for it. The playful simplicity might lead you to trace the movement from the hinge, to the string, to the eye hook, to the shaft, to the wheel, to the crank, to your elbow, to your heart pumping, etc. . . . A merger of art and mechanics.
—Gideon Hughes

Plate 10
Michelle Holzapfel, David Holzapfel,
Donna C. Hawes, Dan MacArthur, Kim Thayer,
Steve Smith, and Brown & Roberts Hardware, all USA
Story Book
2002
American walnut, wild cherry, basswood, curly maple, sugar maple, baltic
birch plywood, parchment, leather, linen, silk, paper, pencil, and ink
15 1/2 x 23 1/4 x 21 1/4 in.

Acknowledgment
is at the heart of this project.
David's photographs tell the story of how
Michelle made the cabinet
and Donna made the books.
It also serves as a record of the
collaboration with family, friends,
neighbors, and business associates.
This is only the beginning of the cabinet's story.
You, the viewers, are invited to participate in
this Cabinet of Curiosity—
and contribute to its history.
Please add your signature and comments
to the Guest Book. Thank you.
—Michelle Holzapfel, November 25, 2002, Marlboro, Vermont

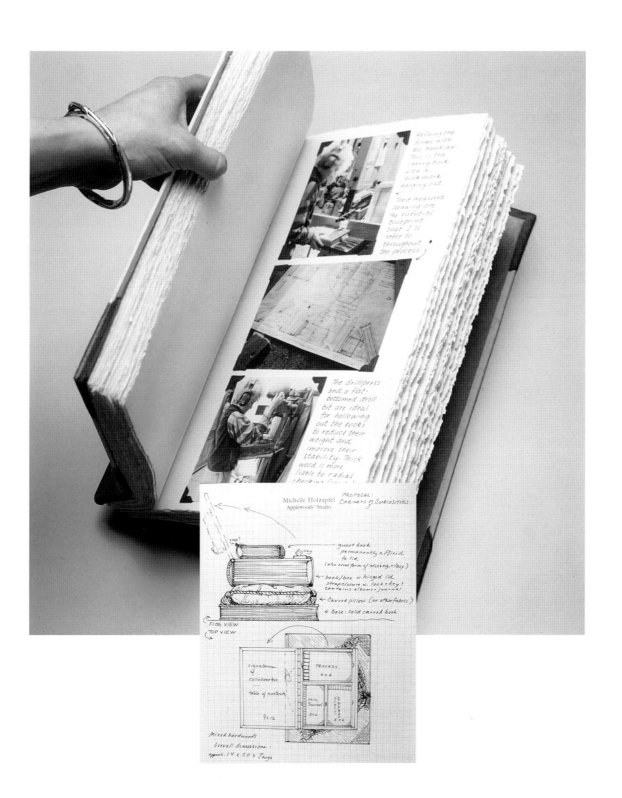

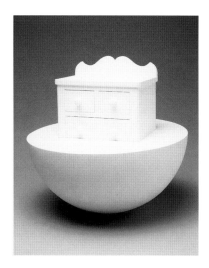

Plate 11

Gordon Peteran, Canada
Chest in a Bowl
2002
Willow
20 x 22 x 22 in.

One day a furniture maker met a turner half way.

This encounter initiated a conversation that exists at the threshold between two construction processes, one additive-one subtractive.

Although the carcase of this mid 19th-century chest wiggles slightly within its host, it does not seem to be able to fully escape from the bowl's embrace. All of the drawers are dove-tailed and detailed with knobs, but the bowl's interior allows only the top two the freedom to open. I'm not sure if this cabinet's plunge into this vessel's volume is a friendly or an adversarial encounter, but full access to both is obscured by their corresponding partner/opponent. Whether a seduction or an intrusion, they are forever bound by the singular paper thin plane that divides them. This relentless/reluctant relationship will present an alternate approach to causing and viewing interior and exterior volume as it relates to curiosities and/or cabinets.

—Gordon Peteran

Plate 12

Michael Hosaluk, Canada; Mitch Ryerson, USA
Round Guy Meets Square Guy
2002
Maple, anigre, western red cedar, acrylic gel, oil and acrylic paint
77 x 24 x 14 in.

Making this piece is an exploration of the unpredictable. This is what makes the idea exciting. A round guy and a square guy have agreed to jump off two cliffs at the same time so they can meet at the bottom. The only possible reason they would try this is because they're curious to see what would happen.

The form we have proposed (loosely) is a possible scenario for what happens at the bottom of the cliff. The shapes meet. The round ones are curious and dance around the square ones. The square ones want to contain the round ones, to support them. A curious relationship is born.

—Michael Hosaluk, Mitch Ryerson

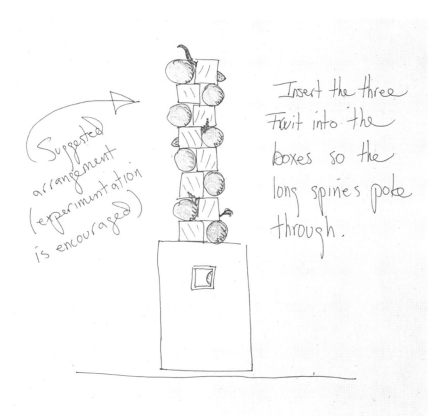

Suggested arrangement (experimentation is encouraged)

Insert the three fruit into the boxes so the long spines poke through.

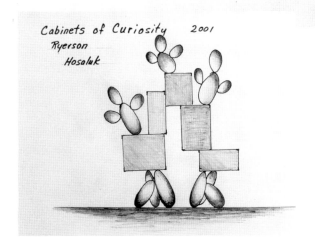

Cabinets of Curiosity   2001
Ryerson
Hosaluk

Plate 13

Miguel Gomez-Ibañez and Joseph Reed, USA
Vargueño
2002
Walnut, ebonized walnut, mother of pearl, purpleheart, ebony, and leather
55 x 31 x 24 in.

Evidence of over 500 years of collaboration between two closely related crafts, the vargueño illustrates historic ties between joiners and turners. But because I do the turnings for my own furniture, I have chosen to collaborate for this exhibition not with a turner, but with a painter. Joseph W. Reed, a painter and longtime friend will contribute 26 small oil paintings, representing the letters A through Z, each including a painted flower, the name of which begins with that letter of the alphabet. The 26 flowers depicted in the botanical alphabet are the "collection" for this cabinet. As I wrote in the original proposal, alphabetizing is a fundamental system for organizing a collection, and the flowers illustrate that idea. The objects that can be contained inside are those selected or treasured by the cabinet's owner, not the maker. I had originally thought I would make my own selection of curious objects, but they would not be important to the concept of the cabinet. It seems clearer to focus attention on the flowers as the collection, and it avoids the need for viewers to open the drawers and inspect the contents in order to understand the work.

—Miguel Gomez-Ibañez

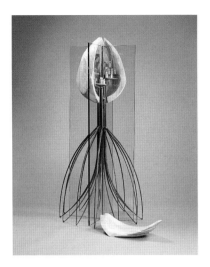

Plate 14

Jack Larimore, USA; Stephen Hogbin, Canada
Seeds of Curiosity: Staples of Transformation
2002
Wood, glass, steel, and cereal seeds
56 x 26 x 26 in.

Jack Larimore and Stephen Hogbin Email Exchange 11/24/01 4:46:48 PM Central Standard Time

Stephen, Sorry for the lapse in communication. . . . My guess is that we'll be e-mailing back and forth for the next few days and then you'll end up writing the proposal and I'll end up doing a sketch. . . . Thoughts about the content: Fragment refers to a part separated from the whole. Separated through a morphing process or through a dissective/analytical process?

I like the reference to cubism, which in this context makes me think about abstracting a metamorphic process . . . it's the relationship between the fragments that makes the piece, not the composition of them.
—Jack Larimore

There is a difference between fragmentary and fragments. Fragmentary refers to a break up of composition whereas fragments may be reordered individual parts, elements, units, modules and patterns are a fragment of the whole. What is a cabinet? The project seems like rather old thinking, a sort of pigeon holing and disconnecting stuff from life. On disPLAY and out of PLAY. "Curiosities" suggests something out of context and therefore loses its meaning developing mystery in a rather artificial manner. "Curiosity" on the other hand is the "desire to know." It interests me how a word can carry very different meanings. It's the same with fragments. Webster is worth reading to get the full meaning(s) of curiosity. Is there a creative way of thinking about a cabinet? A cabinet is loaded with things. Is there a way the box and contents are one and the same thing?
—Stephen Hogbin

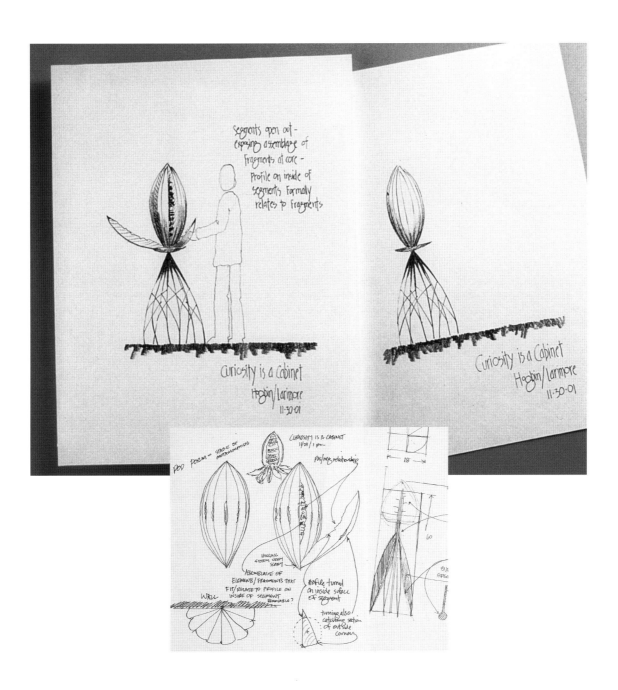

Index

Key to Cover Image Details:

Plate 7	Plate 6	Plate 5	Plate 4	Plate 3	Plate 2	Plate 1
Plate 14	Plate 13	Plate 12	Plate 11	Plate 10	Plate 9	Plate 8

Wood Turning Center
501 Vine Street
Philadelphia, PA 19106
Phone: 215.923.8000
Fax: 215.923.4403
www.woodturningcenter.org

The FURNITURE SOCIETY

The Furniture Society
111 Grovewood Road
Asheville, NC 28804
Phone: 828.255.1949
Fax: 828.255.1950
www.furnituresociety.org